Cambridge E

T0277156

Elements in Shakespea.
edited by
W. B. Worthen
Barnard College

SHAKESPEAREAN CHARITY AND THE PERILS OF REDEMPTIVE PERFORMANCE

Todd Landon Barnes
Ramapo College of New Jersey

CAMBRIDGE
UNIVERSITY PRESS

CAMBRIDGE
UNIVERSITY PRESS

University Printing House, Cambridge CB2 8BS, United Kingdom

One Liberty Plaza, 20th Floor, New York, NY 10006, USA

477 Williamstown Road, Port Melbourne, VIC 3207, Australia

314–321, 3rd Floor, Plot 3, Splendor Forum, Jasola District Centre,
New Delhi – 110025, India

79 Anson Road, #06–04/06, Singapore 079906

Cambridge University Press is part of the University of Cambridge.

It furthers the University's mission by disseminating knowledge in the pursuit of
education, learning, and research at the highest international levels of excellence.

www.cambridge.org
Information on this title: www.cambridge.org/9781108743167
DOI: 10.1017/9781108785716

First published 2020

A catalogue record for this publication is available from the British Library.

ISBN 978-1-108-74316-7 Paperback
ISSN 2516-0109 (print)
ISSN 2516-0117 (online)

Shakespearean Charity and the Perils of Redemptive Performance

Elements in Shakespeare Performance

DOI: 10.1017/9781108785716
First published online: March 2020

Todd Landon Barnes
Ramapo College of New Jersey
Author for correspondence: Todd Landon Barnes, toddbarnes@ramapo.edu

ABSTRACT: This Element examines recent documentaries depicting marginalized youth who are ostensibly redeemed by their encounters with Shakespeare. These films emerge in response to four historical and discursive developments: the rise of reality television and its emphasis on the emotional transformation of the private individual; the concomitant rise of neoliberalism and emotional capitalism, which employ therapeutic discourses to individualize social inequality; the privatization of public education and the rise of so-called "no-excuses" or "new paternalist" charter schools; and the emergence of new modes of address infusing evangelical conversion narratives with a therapeutic self-help ethos.

KEYWORDS: Shakespeare, documentary, education, performance, neoliberalism

ISBNs: 9781108743167 (PB), 9781108785716 (OC)
ISSNs: 2516-0117 (online), 2516-0109 (print)

Contents

Introduction

In the 1990s, audiences appeared to have an undying appetite for Shakespearean drama on the big screen. However, the great Shakespeare boom of the 1990s did not last, and the first decade of the twenty-first century witnessed a big-screen bust as Shakespeare migrated to the small screen. This wasn't, however, merely a change in venue; it was also a change in genre. Filmic adaptations of the plays gave way, in the middle of this first decade, to an inundation of television documentaries about teaching Shakespeare to "at-risk" youth. In Al Pacino's relatively early documentary *Looking for Richard* (1996), what might be considered an urtext for this new genre, Pacino and his colleague Frederic Kimball ask strangers on the street what they think about Shakespeare as they rehearse *Richard III*. One man replies that, though he's an avid watcher of television, he has never actually seen a Shakespeare play. Kimball answers, "That's because there's no Shakespeare on TV!" This is by no means the case today. How do we account for this bust and migration? What happens when Shakespeare moves to the small screen? *Shakespearean Charity and the Perils of Redemptive Performance* takes up a series of television documentaries, all of which depict young people laboring with Shakespearean performance, in order to ask, along with Nietzsche, the genealogical question "what was really happening when that happened?" (41). What were the conditions of possibility, the structures of feeling, that gave rise to this new partnership between Shakespeare, marginalized youth, and the television documentary?

In the pages that follow, I argue that these films emerge in response to four historical and discursive developments: the rise of reality television and its emphasis on the emotional transformation of the private individual; the concomitant rise of neoliberalism and emotional capitalism, which fuses the figure of *homo economicus* with that of *homo sentimentalis*, and which employs therapeutic discourses demanding self-optimization through emotional labor in order to individualize social inequality; the privatization of public education, the rise of so-called "no-excuses" charter schools, the 2001 and 2015 reauthorizations of the 1965 Elementary and Secondary Education Act (ESEA), the ESEA's investments in moral or "character education" and what neoliberal reformers call "the new paternalism," reforms that further dismantle the welfare state while stigmatizing and disciplining the poor; and the emergence of new modes of address that infuse evangelical conversion narratives with a therapeutic self-help ethos. When these forces attach themselves to Shakespeare, we end up with what I call the "White Christian Shakespeare Complex."

The White Christian Shakespeare Complex is a species of what Teju Cole has termed the "White Savior Industrial Complex." Cole, in *The Atlantic* and on Twitter, critiqued the efforts of the Kony 2012 campaign against Joseph Kony, a Ugandan war criminal. For those who don't remember, Kony 2012 was a cloyingly evangelical piece of viral video slacktivism that melted the hearts and fired up the spirits of white middle-class suburban college students around the world. This fervor was matched only by its backlash. The video, which currently has more than 100 million views on YouTube, polarized viewers. Cole wrote the following:

> The white savior supports brutal policy decisions in the morning, founds charities in the afternoon, and receives awards in the evening. The banality of evil transmutes into the banality of sentimentality. The world is nothing but a problem to be solved by enthusiasm. This world exists simply to satisfy the needs – including, importantly, the sentimental needs – of white people and Oprah. The White Savior Industrial Complex is not about justice. It is about having a big emotional experience that validates privilege ... I deeply respect American sentimentality, the way one respects a wounded hippo. You must keep an eye on it, for you know it is deadly.

As a first-generation college student, as a scholarship student whose life was, some might say, saved by Shakespeare, and as someone who has taught Shakespeare to marginalized youth, I was inspired by Cole's comments to ask serious questions about arts education and applied drama's dependency upon its own privilege. It's complicated: How has Shakespeare been used, like the Kony 2012 video, to create "a big emotional experience that validates privilege"? Whose emotions and "sentimental needs"? Whose privilege? What does it mean to give Shakespeare as a gift, and how do we expect students to properly receive Shakespeare? What problems are solved by their enthusiasm?

In her aptly titled *Applied Drama: The Gift of Theatre*, Helen Nicholson notes the dual nature of the gift of theater, reminding us that "there is always a need to be vigilant about whether the practice is accepted as a generous exercise of care or whether, however well-intentioned, it is regarded as an invasive act or unwelcome intrusion. It is easy for trust to become dependency, for generosity to be interpreted as patronage, for interest in others to be experienced as the gaze of surveillance" (166). Operating under the material constraints and logic of what has been called "philanthrocapitalism," all of the films studied here depict philanthropic practices that risk being received as patronizing intrusions. While I do not doubt the benevolence of these practitioners' intentions, I am concerned about the unintended effects of their practices, effects that may in fact form a crucial part of their appeal. As Jenny Hughes and Helen Nicholson note, applied theater's need for funding and its need to produce results – by getting marginalized students into the center – "can mean that applied theater is conceptualized in ways that serve neoliberalism well," even if this recuperation is also "obscured by an apparently activist rhetoric: applied theatre transforms, promotes well-being, improves quality of life, and moves people on" (4). I want to highlight the importance of the therapeutic language evoked here and the way such imperatives to attain emotional health can work in the service of neoliberalization.

In what follows, I argue that the films in question, and the practices documented within them, serve and reflect larger projects of neoliberalization. While at times I may invoke neoliberalism as an historical period, as it has been sketched out by scholars such as David Harvey in his *Brief History of Neoliberalism*, or while neoliberalism might instead name a set of policy innovations associated with the Mont Pelerin Society or Chicago School economics, innovations largely introduced to humanities scholars through the work of Michel Foucault, I largely follow the definition proposed by Wendy Brown, who, in her recent book *Undoing the Demos: Neoliberalism's Stealth Revolution*, acknowledges that "neoliberalism as economic policy, a mode of governance, and an order of reason is at once a global phenomenon, yet inconsistent, differentiated, unsystematic, impure ... It is globally ubiquitous, yet disunified and nonidentical with itself in space and time"

(20–21). Nevertheless, in her chapter on the neoliberalization of higher education, Brown focuses her attention on neoliberalism as a rationality or "order of reason." She writes:

> [Neoliberalism] is best understood not simply as economic policy, but as a governing rationality that disseminates market values and metrics to every sphere of life and construes the human itself exclusively as *homo oeconomicus*. Neoliberalism thus does not merely privatize – turn over to the market for individual production and consumption – what was formerly publicly supported and valued. Rather, it formulates everything, everywhere in terms of capital investment and appreciation, including and especially humans themselves (176).

Leigh Claire La Berge and Quinn Slobodian have found Brown's pronouncements on neoliberalism's triumph and ubiquity too totalizing and a bit premature, even if Brown herself highlights how inconsistencies within the neoliberal imaginary might serve to caution us against reading her narrative as "a teleological one, a dark chapter in a steady march toward end times" (La Berge and Slobodian 611; Brown 21). For this reason, at times I use "neoliberalization" in order to index the incomplete, heterogeneous, and continuous nature of neoliberal reforms. More importantly for this project, recent scholarship stresses how, contrary to (and yet compatible with) laissez-faire models of capitalism, neoliberalization refigures the state as a crucial market actor, relying upon the "active intervention of what neoliberals often called the 'visible hand' of law, state, and … religion to encase and protect capital rights" (La Berge and Slobodian 606). Further, contrary to critiques of neoliberalism that focus exclusively on society's reduction to the individual market actor, the works of Wendy Brown and Melinda Cooper more accurately argue that "it is the reproductive family unit, not the individual, that is the basic unit of the neoliberal imaginary" (606). For these reasons, throughout this project I highlight the changing roles of the family, the state, and religion in these films.

While Shakespeare studies has focused on the many pedagogical uses of filmed dramatizations of Shakespeare's plays in the classroom, very few take on these documentary films, which embed this very problematic within their diegesis. Only through an attentiveness to the institutional and discursive context of these films can we see how they operate to solidify Shakespeare's place in relation to the White Christian Shakespeare Complex, a complex that, I argue, interpellates marginalized youth into a particularly neoliberal, patriarchal, and puritanical vision of capitalism.

All of these films provoke and document emotion by combining reversals of cultural fortune with transformations in the emotional "health" of poor students, many of whom are, importantly, students of color – though few films address this fact. In *Shakespeare High* (2011), for example, we meet Luis Gueta, a former gang member turned thespian, or, in his words, a "big badass cholo ni**er" turned "motherfucking geek." Upon winning first place for his performance in *Midsummer Night's Dream*, he explains his motivation: "What we needed to do is to stand up as an example. We don't have to be white, and we don't have to be rich, yeah, you know, coming from the bottom, we're the underdogs." Paula Hunter, the drama teacher at Hesperia High School, a rural desert school in which, we learn, "most of these kids have separated parents," similarly remarks, "I always think of [Hesperia] as the underdog." Much of the appeal of these films' engagement with the White Christian Shakespeare Complex is the appeal of the underdog narrative, though such underdogs are never explicitly marked by race or class. Furthermore, if these films show us "underdogs" who become emotionally healthy and culturally rich, they do not challenge or depict the structures that made them unhealthy or poor to begin with. Theodor Adorno sums up the dangers of these films best when he warns, "In the end, glorification of splendid underdogs is nothing other than glorification of the splendid system that makes them so" (28). The same might be said for the glorification of those who facilitate the underdogs' transformation, be they teachers, arts educators, actors, therapists, or life coaches.

In the final moments of *Kings of Baxter: Can Twelve Teenage Offenders Conquer Macbeth?* (2017), a film in which two professional actors try to motivate disinclined incarcerated youth to perform *Macbeth*, Huw McKinnon, an actor with Bell Shakespeare, Australia's national theater company, seems close to acknowledging the central problematic of the White Christian Shakespeare Complex. No other film makes such an acknowledgment, and here it happens very quickly, under McKinnon's breath, and within faltering syntax and a strange piece of Australian slang. After complimenting and encouraging a panicked – or just unmotivated – actor on the eve of the performance, McKinnon, exasperated, tells the camera, "It's a real fine line between being in his face too much . . . I'm also conscious of pissing in his pocket, like, when they know when you . . . you know what I mean?" To "piss in one's pocket," an abbreviated form of "to piss in one's pocket and tell one it's raining," according to Urban Dictionary and my Australian friends, means "to insincerely attempt to convince a person that you're doing them a favor, when you actually have only your own interest (generally making a profit or ingratiating oneself) at heart."[1] McKinnon seems to partially acknowledge, here, the fact that the youth in the film – barely invested in the project all along – "know when you" are manipulating them and how much emotional labor they're really performing for their ostensible donors. At two points in the film both parties quip that they know the teens are performing only for the candy they receive for showing up to rehearsal. Though it's never directly acknowledged, nevertheless, everyone in the film seems to know that their endeavor is a failure, and it's perhaps this inadvertent proximity to honesty and failure that is *Kings of Baxter*'s greatest achievement as a film. Unlike so many of these films, *Kings of Baxter* refuses to deploy what Lauren Berlant has called "cruel optimism"; the film never figures Shakespeare as an attachment that might provide redemption or "the good life" under neoliberal conditions of precarity (*Cruel Optimism* 1).

Act I of *Othello* offers a scene that I find emblematic of the documentaries examined here. There, we witness an autobiographical tale within an autobiographical tale, as Othello delivers his "round and unvarnished tale" to the Venetian Senate. Autobiography and documentary, as I hope to show, as modes of storytelling, share a similarly fraught relationship to the private truths they construct yet pretend to merely reveal. Within Othello's tale, he recounts being continually asked by Brabantio, and then by Desdemona herself, to tell the "story of [his] life," particularly of its "disastrous chances" and "hairbreadth scapes i'th' imminent-deadly breach," of being "sold to slavery," and his "redemption thence." Such imperatives seem to mirror the demands these documentaries make of their participants. The institutional imperative to recount one's triumph over adversity is also, it's worth noting, a commonplace

[1] The OED's definition of this phrase seems less apt than the one found in Urban Dictionary.

of college and scholarship application essay prompts. Othello tells tales of exotic spaces far removed from Venice, piquing the voyeuristic – if not imperialist – impulses of his interlocutors. Desdemona, distracted, would "seriously incline" and with a "greedy ear / Devour up [his] discourse." This tale "beguile[s] her of her tears" when he speaks "of some distressful stroke / That [his] youth suffered" (1.3.130–159). Much is made of the power of this tale to woo, to forge love and pity, in the broadest sense, between two people. Even the telling of the telling of the tale moves the Duke. In relation to the Shakespearean documentaries I examine here, this familiar scene speaks in new ways by pointedly indexing the emotional powers, racial dimensions, uneven relations, and discursive contours of Shakespearean charity and redemptive performance.

Othello tells the Duke, "She loved me for the dangers I had passed / And I loved her that she did pity them" (1.3.168–169). Desdemona's "pity," an ambivalent and capacious affective relation in the early modern imaginary, if not within our own today, seems emblematic of the ambivalent role of emotion in these films. We might read her exchange with Othello sympathetically, as a moment of intercultural affection balanced by the fact that Othello is able to tell his own story, his testimony, and not have it told by others who might "extenuate / [Or] set down aught in malice" (5.2.340–341). In this reading, the affective exchange is a fair one, even if emotional exchange is cast in the language of the market: "She gave me for my pains a world of sighs" (1.3.160). Reading this scene more cynically, however, we might imagine Othello, both in court and in courtship, engaged in asymmetrical emotional and rhetorical labor, downplaying his skills and speaking upon hints while telling stories he knows his audiences want to hear. The documentaries in question share this ambivalence, and while they may purport to have good intentions, I want to read the practices depicted – and their very depiction – with a measured balance of cynicism and sympathy.

1 Genre Trouble: Between Fiction, Documentary, and Reality Television

Why did big-box-office, big-screen Shakespearean drama give way to low-budget, documentary television Shakespeare in the early 2000s? First, we should note that this shift occurs within the very years that documentary, in general and on the big screen, was achieving mainstream box-office success. Documentary figures like Michael Moore, Errol Morris, and Al Gore were attaining unprecedented mainstream appeal and some of the biggest box-office records for documentaries to date. Steven Mintz argues, "The most stunning development in movies in the early twenty-first century is the surging popularity of the documentary … Seven of the all-time Top 10 grossing documentaries were released in 2003 and 2004, and 18 of the 25 most profitable political documentaries were released since 2002" (10). Jonathan Kahana tells us that Moore's *Bowling for Columbine* in 2002 inaugurated a boom in documentary, but that this boom, however, quickly went bust: "Since 2004, the year that *Fahrenheit 9/11* led a cycle of politically themed documentaries into theaters, total domestic box office for documentary had dropped steadily, from $171 million in 2004 to $116 million the following year, to $55 million in 2006, and only $2 million at the midway point of 2007" (*Intelligence Work* 327). The first wave of Shakespearean documentaries – *A Touch of Greatness: A Portrait of a Maverick Teacher* (2004), *My Shakespeare: Romeo and Juliet for a New Generation with Baz Luhrmann* (2004), *Why Shakespeare?* (2005), *The Hobart Shakespeareans* (2005), *Shakespeare Behind Bars* (2005), *Ballet Changed My Life: Ballet Hoo!* (2006), and *Mickey B* (2007) – appeared, significantly, during this boom, though only *Shakespeare Behind Bars* appeared in wide release on the big screen.

We might also point out that this rise of the documentary coincided with a larger destabilization of truth under the Bush administration – beginning with the disputed election in 2000 – and a paranoid truth-seeking in the wake of the terror attacks of September 11, 2001, as evidenced by the so-called 9/11 truther movement. Kahana notes that, while much attention has been given to big-screen documentaries of this period, especially presidential political documentaries, "the more interesting phenomenon was the distribution of documentary themes and dispositions across various levels of culture" (*Intelligence Work* 328). He points to the growing number of documentaries appearing on small screens at that time. This sudden increase of small-screen documentaries, importantly, coincides with the emergence and triumph of "prestige television." In the second decade of the twenty-first century, we have witnessed a continuation of Shakespearean pedagogical documentaries: *When Romeo Met Juliet* (2010), *Shakespeare High* (2011), *Fame High: The Talented Students at the Los Angeles County High School for the Arts* (2012), *Caesar Must Die* (2013), *Romeo Is Bleeding* (2015), *Midsummer in Newton* (2016), and *Kings of Baxter: Can Twelve Teenage Offenders Conquer Macbeth?* (2017).[2] All of these films, to varying degrees, and in very different ways, argue for Shakespeare's power to "transform" or "redeem" poor students, most of whom are students of color. In fact, watching these films feels in many ways like watching the same film over and over, a repetition that must index an urgent social anxiety around the intersections of class, race, education, and documentary. Such repetitions make sense given Kahana's claim that documentary functions according to a logic of allegory, wherein "documentary representation both depends upon and displaces the particular value of the individual case, affirming its value in the name of an abstract principle" (*Intelligence Work* 8). What abstract principle do the displaced individual lives surveyed in these films affirm? In order to find out, we will proceed allegorically, moving between specific moments in these films and a broader examination of their shared abstract principles. My hope, however, is that we need not displace the particular in favor of the general.

Film scholars have long noted a significant change in late twentieth-century documentary style, from a *cinéma-vérité* or direct cinema style to one that borrows elements of the fiction film. Conversely, the fiction film can now be seen borrowing elements of the documentary. Linda Williams, in her discussion of Oliver Stone's *JFK* and Errol Morris's *The Thin Blue Line*, suggests that

---

[2] Though an examination of prison Shakespeare documentaries (e.g., *Shakespeare behind Bars*, *Mickey B*, *Caesar Must Die*, and *Jail Caesar*) is beyond the scope of this Element – and is explored fully elsewhere – the prison industrial complex haunts the White Christian Shakespeare Complex, if for no other reason than that we cannot consider schools separately from prisons, given the school-to-prison pipeline, a phenomenon masterfully explored in Anna Deavere Smith's *Notes from the Field* (play, 2015; film, 2018). It's also worth noting that all of the disciplinary institutions examined by Foucault – schools, prisons, hospitals and mental institutions, and army barracks – serve as sites for recent Shakespearean documentary films.

the "historical fiction film borrowing many aspects of the form of documentary" might be contrasted with "what we might call the low-budget postmodern documentary borrowing many features of the fiction film" (796). Kahana adds, "In a manner that was soon imitated widely, Morris embraced cinematic artifice, incorporating techniques of performance, of cinematography, and *mise-en-scène*, of musical scoring, and of editing that were anathema to the reportorial ethos of *cinéma vérité*" ("Introduction" 723). As these genres bleed into each other, we notice a surprising number of fiction films about the production of a Shakespearean drama – e.g., *In the Bleak Midwinter* (1995), *Shakespeare in Love* (1998), or television's *Slings and Arrows* (2003–2006) – that share the audition-rehearsal-performance structure found in Shakespearean documentaries (Purcell 538). We might consider how Shakespeare's own dramas, particularly the history plays, have long engaged in a similar cross-genre borrowing. The most recent big-budget (£9 million) screen adaptation of Shakespeare's plays is, notably, Sam Mendes's *The Hollow Crown* series (2012–2016) (Morse 7). This adaptation of the *Henriad* (both tetralogies), however, put historical drama on the small screen, airing on BBC and then on PBS.

In addition to these formal borrowings, we must attend to the way in which these Shakespearean documentaries borrow subject matter, narrative patterns, and tropes from the fiction films that preceded them, particularly within the decades-long genre of the working-class classroom drama: *Blackboard Jungle* (1955), *To Sir, with Love* (1967), *Conrack* (1974), *Stand and Deliver* (1988), *Dangerous Minds* (1995), and *Freedom Writers* (2007), to name just one during each decade. But beyond these films, which deal with education generally, I'd like to observe the prescient particularity of one film, *Renaissance Man* (1994), which fictionalizes the teaching of Shakespeare and establishes the ground upon which the Shakespearean documentary will flourish. *Renaissance Man* follows down-and-out Detroiter Bill Rago (Danny DeVito) as he teaches *Hamlet* and *Henry V* to military recruits "at risk" of being kicked out of the army because they lack "comprehension"; they are referred to as "double Ds," "dumb as dogshit." On the first day of class, the recalcitrant recruits write an autobiographical essay about why they joined the army. They all read aloud their stories of hardship: dead, absent, or laid-off fathers, poverty and hunger, the isolation of life in a trailer park, homelessness, gang violence, and murder. One character, Private Brian Davis Jr. (Peter Simmons), breaks into tears when recounting the tale of his dead father. Once the class is done, Private Donne Benitez (Lillo Brancato Jr.) asks, "That good enough, Mr. Rago?" Mr. Rago nods and quietly replies, "Yeah." Their pains for a world of Rago's sighs.

On the first day of class, we learn that the recruits are from diverse towns across the United States: three are from Detroit, one is from New York City, another is itinerant, one is from Grand Forks, North Dakota, one is from Charlotte, North Carolina, and another is from Willacoochee, Georgia. Four are black, two are poor Southern whites, and one is clearly marked as an urban Italian-American. The ensuing drama works to resolve the classed, raced, and regional tensions exhibited throughout the first part of the film, with the notable exception being the case of Private Nathaniel T. Hobbs, a black recruit who is discovered to have enlisted under false pretenses in order to escape the law, which has been after him for dealing drugs. Later, we see him in his jail cell as he narrates a letter to Mr. Rago. We learn that he's reading *Othello* while incarcerated and that, if the teachers in prison are anything like Mr. Rago, he just might decide to take some college classes. We also learn that Mr. Rago wrote letters to the warden in order to secure Hobbs an early release. In the way the film sets up racial tensions in order for us to watch them melt away as the bonds of compulsory friendship form, the film seems to participate in a longer cinematic tradition of depicting fantasies of racial reconciliation.

Sharon Willis has written extensively about such racial reconciliation fantasies. Focusing on the career of Sidney Poitier, who moves from playing the student in *Blackboard Jungle* to playing the inspirational teacher in *To Sir, with Love*, Willis articulates the endurance of what she calls the "Poitier effect," which "functions as a defense, or a compensatory gesture, averting or deflecting the possibility of a kind of critical thinking that would involve a serious reciprocal interracial exchange, instead offering a fantasy of racial understanding and 'assimilation' that requires no effort on the part of white people" (5). Willis shows how the Poitier effect operates through "stories and epiphanies of radical transformation through intimate pedagogical exchange [that] show themselves especially hospitable to and compatible with the conventions of melodrama" (6). Surveying recent scholarship, Willis shows how the tradition of the racial melodrama appears to take on serious social issues but instead "unfold[s] in isolated environments, where cultural and social conflicts and contradictions become displaced onto individualized, private negotiations" (6), a displacement that forecloses the possibility of critically or historically assessing race relations. *Renaissance Man*, and many of the documentaries studied here, seems to repeat and continue in the tradition of the Poitier effect. In this project, I worry, along with Willis, that "racial melodrama seems condemned to repetition/reenactment rather than working through" (9). To what extent do our films operate as cinematic fantasies of white wish fulfilment?

At the end of *Renaissance Man*, audiences are moved when Private Benitez, egged on by the film's merciless drill instructor (Gregory Hines), is able to recite the entirety of Prince Hal's Saint Crispin's Day speech – Shakespeare, arguably, at his most nationalistic and militaristic. Mr. Rago had recently taken the group to see a performance of *Henry V*. In the film's final moments, the entire group volunteers to take Mr. Rago's Shakespeare test, and it is clear that they all pass (save Pvt. Hobbs). All of these tropes – student testimonials on the adversity their youth suffered, the exposure of diverse, underprivileged, and underprepared students to Shakespeare, racial tensions eased by a new sense of community, friendship, and "intimate pedagogical exchange," the moment when anxious students publicly demonstrate their comprehension of and love for Shakespeare, and finally, strangely, the triumphant recitation of Hal's speech – all figure prominently in the documentary films of the twenty-first century.

Another problem of genre presents itself if we notice how nearly all of these new Shakespearean documentaries seem indebted to the rise and subsequent ubiquity of reality television, a genre as popular in the United States as it is in the United Kingdom. *Shakespeare High*, which depicts students from diverse schools (charter, private, public, urban, rural, suburban) competing in the Drama Teachers Association of Southern California's Shakespeare Festival, is explicitly structured around a contest, with its judges and first, second, and third place winners. In this, it shares the structure and emotional tensions of the game show–reality television hybrid genre known as "gamedoc" (Murray 67). Most of these films are structured around the labor of auditions, rehearsal, and self-improvement, leading up to the emotional revelation of their talents on opening night, aligning them with the genre of reality television called the "docusoap." As Susan Greenhalgh and Robert Shaughnessy have shown, writing about *My Shakespeare*, "The set-up, and the film's three-part structure (auditioning in the midst of local indifference, rehearsal and its tribulations, and eventual performance), adopt the industry-standard template of performance-related 'docusoaps'" (91). The docusoap is a part of the "legacy of direct cinema (also called observational or cinéma verité)" (Murray 67). Nearly all seem to fuse competition with emotion and labor. Though many of these films aired on PBS in the United States and on Channel 4 or the BBC in the United Kingdom, and though many were funded by the US National Endowment for the Arts (NEA), and others were supported by or associated with the Royal Academy of Dramatic Art, the Birmingham Royal Opera, or Bell Shakespeare in Australia, the affective and emotional contours of these films seem to deploy and yet undercut any claim to the "discourses of sobriety" associated with early documentary film in the tradition of John Grierson (Nichols 3).

In many ways, contemporary documentary and reality television have much in common. Both direct cinema and reality TV fixate on "the mundane, the everyday, the personal . . . the intimate" (Murray 68). In this way, particularity is linked to generality. In *Shakespeare High*, for example, we meet Chris "VATO" Marquez as he walks us through his family's studio apartment, where he sleeps on the floor because his brother, who has Down's syndrome, needs to sleep on the couch. The camera lingers on the couch, the bed, and the place on the floor where Marquez sleeps – five family members in a studio apartment. In *Romeo Is Bleeding*, we see the insides of the students' homes. We see D'Neise Robinson's kitchen as she examines the family refrigerator and engages her mom in an argument about the lack of food. In *Kings of Baxter*, where the faces of the incarcerated youth are blurred to protect their identity, the camera instead slowly pans across each boy's cell; in lieu of faces, we see metonyms of identity: bars of soap, shampoo, magazines, an eraser, a deck of cards (see Figure 1).

The distinction between reality television and contemporary documentary further erodes when we examine distribution and reception. According to Susan Murray, in her study of reality television shows and documentaries that have been repackaged as they migrate between various low- and high-brow studios (Fox, PBS, and HBO), "[m]uch of our evaluative process is based on

Figure 1 Metonyms of identity in *Kings of Baxter* (2017)

the belief that documentaries should be educational or informative, authentic, ethical, socially engaged, independently produced, and serve the public interest, while reality TV programs are commercial, sensational, entertaining, and potentially exploitative and/or manipulative" (67–68). However, the "dialectic" between documentary and reality TV, as Murray terms it and as we can see in these films, can even work to mystify or disguise the exploitation or manipulation of works we imagine to be "pure" observational documentary. For that reason, I think it's necessary to consider the possibility that the films in question are as exploitative, as manipulative, and as commercial as reality television, as well as less informative, less authentic, and less socially engaged than their various institutional or instructional pedigrees might suggest. Murray highlights how the "distinctions we make between forms of nonfictional television are not based on empirical evidence but largely contained in the evaluative connotations that insist on separating information from entertainment, liberalism from sensationalism, and public service from commercialism" (79). In a world in which these distinctions are each eroding, a world of "relatable" edutainment, ostensibly "fake news," and public-private partnerships, our Shakespearean pedagogy films also seem suspended in a new (yet recycled), hybrid (yet often quite simple), generic and political terrain. Furthermore, in this new global media landscape, Shakespearean pedagogical documentaries blur national distinctions, as online streaming and repackaging (e.g., BBC content aired on PBS or streamed online from anywhere) make such programs readily available on either side of the Atlantic. For this reason, though my project focuses primarily on US films, significant attention is given to UK productions released during the tenure of New Labour, a time in which parallel cultural and market reforms and pressures produced an increased demand for Shakespearean charity and redemptive performance.

Maggie Nelson reminds us of what should be obvious in thinking about Shakespearean charity and the perils of redemptive performance, regardless of whether they appear in proper "documentary" film or improper "reality television": "Some of the most good-intentioned, activist, 'compassionate' art out there can end up being patronizing, ineffective, or exploitative" (9). Pooja Rangan further undercuts the claims of the documentary tradition, beginning her book *Immediations: The Humanitarian Impulse in Documentary* by asking, "What does endangered life do for documentary? As practitioners, critics, and spectators of documentary, we rarely ask this question. Instead, we commonly believe that documentary works on behalf of the disenfranchised by 'giving a voice to the voiceless' ... I argue that endangered, dehumanized life not only sustains documentary but supplies its raison d'être" (1). Despite the recent popularity of the liberal or humanitarian documentary, there is a long – largely ignored – history of those who have critiqued the aspirations and effects of such films.

Brian Winston has noticed that, even within the Griersonian documentaries of the interwar years, "[f]actual television ... substitutes empathy for analysis, it privileges effect over cause, and it, therefore, seldom results in any spin-offs in the real world – that is, actions taken in society as a result of the program to ameliorate the conditions depicted" (767–768). Winston cites director Basil Wright, who in 1974 had this to say about his interwar documentary:

> You know this film (*Children in School*) was made in 1937. The other thing is that this film shows up the appalling conditions in the schools in Britain in 1937 which are identical with the ones which came out on television the night before

last: over-crowded classes, schoolrooms falling down, and so
on. It's the same story. That is really terrible, isn't it? (763)

Winston is not alone in his skepticism regarding the power of the documentary, and Rangan is not alone in her fears of the harm caused by "the heirs of Grierson's humanitarian mission" (Rangan 3). Jill Godmilow, herself a documentary filmmaker, holds an equally dim view of documentary's ability to live up to its ostensible mission:

> [T]he progressive or liberal documentary is an inadequate form, a relatively useless cultural product, especially for political change. Its basic strategy is description, and it makes arguments by organizing visual evidence, expressive local testimony and expert technical testimony into a deceptively satisfying emotional form. These standard filmic conventions do little to inform the audience of its own role in socially oppressive relationships and conditions, or to rouse the audience from its implicit complacency with the status quo. (91)

Important to note here is the idea that these documentaries deploy testimony in "a deceptively satisfying emotional form." Susan Sontag was perhaps the greatest critic of the ways in which simply regarding the pain of others holds the potential to short-circuit more substantial forms of aid while providing such voyeurs a means to disavow their connection to others. She writes, "So far as we feel sympathy, we feel we are not accomplices to what caused the suffering. Our sympathy proclaims our innocence as well as our impotence." Such sympathy, for Sontag, prevents us from "reflect[ing] on how our privileges are located on the same map as their suffering, and may – in ways we might prefer not to imagine – be linked to their suffering, as the wealth of some may imply the destitution of others" (102–103).

Like the documentaries Godmilow describes, reality television also substitutes emotional appeals and solutions for examinations or critiques of larger structural failures. The role of emotion is discussed further in the next section, but it's important to note here that a do-good ethos and a feel-good redemption telos also pervade reality television at the turn of the twenty-first century. But reality television does more than document the suffering of marginalized populations; in many cases, reality television, like applied drama, aims to intervene in the emotional, psychological, even economic lives of individual persons. Amber Watts discusses the period between 2003 and 2005, when many of our Shakespearean documentaries premiered:

> [The period between 2003 and 2005] saw the debut of many "feel-good" reality shows that set out to transform their subjects inside and out, while tugging at America's heart-strings ... [programs that] sought to transform real Americans in real need – be it of medical, economic, psychological, or behavioral support – into healthy, attractive, and financially stable citizens ... all these programs framed their subjects' transformations as narratives of misery and redemption, with the shows themselves playing the role of altruistic benefactors to the downtrodden. (301)

According to Ian Wilhelm, this subgenre, which he calls "charity TV," is "part of a growing genre of programs that make doing good – or the appearance of doing good – a key part of their audience appeal" (24). Wilhelm points to *The Secret Millionaire*, in which a disguised donor "lives in a working-class area to find a worthy recipient of almost $100,000" – what could be more Shakespearean? – *Extreme Makeover: Home Edition*, in which builders and designers repair the homes of the destitute, and Donald Trump's collaboration with Autism Speaks (a charity itself condemned by more than sixty disability organizations for "exploiting those it purports to help") on *The Apprentice* (24) (also see Autism Self-Advocacy Network). Wilhelm cites Robert J. Thompson, who locates these shows within the tradition of nineteenth-century "Dickens-era poverty tourism," in which wealthy donors "go to poor houses and watch poor people eat sumptuous Christmas dinners that [donors] helped pay for" (24). This tradition survives and mutates as it continues throughout the twentieth century. Watts draws our attention to how television revives this tradition in the postwar era, when popular "audience participation" shows like *Queen for a Day*,

Strike It Rich, and *High Finance* featured "individuals disclosing real-life troubles on-air"; such individuals were rewarded if they could generate enough sympathy or applause (302, 304). It is clear, then, that twenty-first-century charity TV is part of a much longer tradition, one rooted in the economic disparity and philanthropic ethos of the nineteenth century.

If the early twentieth-century documentaries trained their attention on white, working-class, unionized laborers, the late twentieth and early twenty-first centuries, under conditions of austerity, financial crisis, and neoliberalization, present us with a new form of documentary, one with new participants and new problems. Kahana astutely writes, "The American welfare state was partly defined by the documentary forms that made it seem necessary. A different documentary ideology accompanies the waning of this political imaginary" (*Intelligence Work* 323). In the wake of the 2008 global financial crisis, charity TV suffused cable television, presenting shows like *Pawn Stars* (2009), *Storage Wars* (2010), *Repo Games* (2011), and their various spin-offs. Nick Serpe has highlighted how a "new set of reality shows [that] thrive on foreclosed property and unpaid bills" represent "a distinctly post-recession phenomenon" (15). What's more, the production and form of these new reality shows are also shaped by neoliberalism, as reality television writers are nonunionized and often have poor salaries and benefits (14). Chad Raphael adds that reality television programs "also cut costs by wholeheartedly embracing low-end production values. Direct cinema techniques such as handheld cameras and the use of available lighting made shows . . . particularly cheap" (130). Raphael and others have shown that, in the 1980s and 1990s, attempts to bypass unions by producing reality television led to a series of strikes by the Writers Guild and other unions, strikes that paved the way for reality television and that became "an integral part of the network strategies to control labor unrest" (127–129). Reality TV writers themselves have organized and walked off the job, describing work conditions as "high-status sweatshops" (Verhoeven).

If, in its form and production, reality television indexes the austerity of late capitalism and, as Kahana suggests, an ideology rooted in the decline of the welfare state, the content of the documentaries examined here also does some of the important work in naturalizing neoliberal ideology. Susan

Murray and Laurie Ouellette make a strong case for how reality television stands in, as a therapeutic supplement, for social services gutted by neoliberalization. They argue that "the TV industry has found that there is money to be made by taking on the duties of the philanthropist, the social worker, the benefactor, the 'guardian angel'" (2). Though many of the Shakespearean documentaries of the early twenty-first century aired on public television, the theatrical interventions they depict (in addition to the funding that secured their production) are made not by the state but by individuals and private entities. What's more, their social interventions supplement and thereby threaten to supplant a diminished public support. Ouellette and James Hay describe how "[w]ithin the context of the reinvention of government, TV's concern with not only documenting, but with facilitating the care of needy and 'at-risk' citizens through cultural commerce, philanthropy, and TV-viewer voluntarism is also a way of enacting methods of social service provision that do not involve 'entitlements' and modes of civic participation that do not 'depend' on the Welfare State" (6). I want to consider how reality television, specifically our Shakespearean films, engage in both "documenting" and "facilitating," and how these gestures relate.

A tension exists between the desire to facilitate, on the one hand, and to document, on the other. Alongside their indices of social reality or truth, these Shakespearean documentaries also contain, within their diegesis, social actors – mentors and students – and their uneven engagements with fictional drama. Nearly all of these films are structured around a peculiar double looking. Through the camera's documentary gaze, we watch experts who in turn watch and facilitate a scenario in which amateurs perform emotional drama (literally, on stage, and figuratively, off stage). Claire Bishop, in her discussion of socially engaged, pedagogical, and participatory arts, argues that very "few of these projects manage to overcome the gap between a 'first audience' of student-participants and a 'second audience' of subsequent viewers. Perhaps this is because, ultimately, education has no spectators ... Yet, this task is essential to projects in the artistic realm if they are to fulfil the ambitions of an aesthetic education" (272). This double looking, what Bishop calls "a dual horizon," operates like a play-within-a-play, and it's like no other play-within-a-play more than the "rude mechanicals'" sub-amateur performance of *Pyramus and Thisbe* for their social betters in *A Midsummer Night's Dream* (*MND*) (274).

Like our documentaries, *MND* adheres to the "gamedoc" format in which auditions and turbulent rehearsals are followed by a competition and a performance. In our documentaries, as in *MND*, this "dual horizon" is also classed: poor and working-class amateur actors perform in the most impressive venues and for the most dignified audiences – a reversal of contemporary audience-performer power dynamics and a return to the dynamic of early modern court performances. In *The Hobart Shakespeareans* and *Why Shakespeare?* we see immigrant fifth graders from Los Angeles perform for a largely millionaire Congress in the US Capitol; in *Ballet Changed My Life*, poor "at-risk" youth work with life coaches and the Birmingham Royal Ballet in order to perform alongside professionals in Birmingham's Hippodrome; in *My Shakespeare: Romeo and Juliet for a New Generation with Baz Luhrmann*, the eponymous director "mentors" professional actor Patterson Joseph (only via satellite, never in person) as the latter recruits and rehearses with a group of black teens from Harlesden (a neighborhood in northwest London Joseph describes as "one of the least likeliest places to have Shakespeare"), preparing them to perform at the Royal Academy of Dramatic Art (one of the most likely); and in *Shakespeare High*, "underserved" students from the Partnership to Uplift Communities (PUC) Community Charter Early College High School – what a name! – compete against and defeat students from the wealthiest private schools in Los Angeles. PUC Charter wins the competition, of course, by performing as the "rude mechanicals." We might also note that these students win first place for comedy, and unlike the student groups from wealthier schools, we never once see them perform tragedy. While many find the representation of the Athenian tradesmen, generally, or Nick Bottom, in particular, sympathetic, one must completely ignore – or fully accept – the way class functions in the play in order to do so. *MND* is structured around a deep ambivalence: Do we laugh *with* Bottom or *at* him? Is the play an innocent and loveable romp, or is loving a play featuring a date-rape drug, violations of sexual consent, and bullying the poor more akin to being woo'd by Theseus's sword? Again, we can be "sympathetic" (perhaps without any sympathy for Bottom, Titania, or Hippolyta) or cynical.

Feminist readings of the play have allowed us to see the misogyny of the play anew, but surprisingly few have explored the class elements mystified by the play's pastoral-comical element.[3] Kenneth Burke is an important exception. Burke crucially observes how comedy has the power to turn a "social psychosis" in the world outside of the play into "*entertainment*" within the play. Burke pointedly asks "about a possible 'social psychosis' that underlies [the Athenian tradesmen's] masque-like comedy, doubtless written originally for appreciation 'from the top down.'" He locates this social psychosis, what he later calls a "courtly psychosis," in the obvious: "intense conflict between social classes" (179, 178). While casual viewers of ostensibly "low-brow" reality television might easily observe that its stock-in-trade consists of transforming social psychoses into entertainment, liberal Shakespearean documentaries like *Shakespeare High* are no exception; though they make us *feel good*, they too participate in a similar transformation.[4]

When Theseus is warned that the play within the play, crafted by "Hard-handed men ... Which never labored in their minds till now" "Made [Philostrate's] eyes water; but more merry tears / The passion of loud laughter never shed," Theseus pats himself on the back, explaining that "The kinder we, to give them thanks for nothing" (5.1.72–5.1.73; 5.1.69–5.1.70; 5.1.89). Despite Hippolyta's claim, in solidarity with the amateurs, that she "love[s] not to see wretchedness o'ercharged," Theseus replies that "love ... and tongue-tied simplicity ... speak most, to [his] capacity" (5.1.85; 5.1.104–105). Why does his "capacity" desire their "love" and "tongue-tied simplicity"? Why does he, and why do viewers of these documentaries, love to see wretchedness overcharged? Is something like charity TV at work here? When does one person's tragedy become another's comedy?

---

[3] For just one example of such a feminist reading, see Sanchez, "'Use Me But as Your Spaniel.'"

[4] Worth noting here is another exception: hotel heiress Paris Hilton's reality show *The Simple Life* shows us what such a transformation of courtly psychosis might look like when its typical class positions are reversed. In this show, the privileged are lampooned as they attempt to do manual labor on a farm; however, as Jennifer L. Pozner notes, in this show, which she and others have described as "*Beverly Hillbillies* in reverse," the rural workers are also, often, the butt of the joke.

Sukanta Chaudhuri puts it bluntly: "the ['rude mechanicals'] are rank amateurs putting on a show in honour of their overlords" (4). Shakespeare's plays, with their many plays within plays, dramatize a relationship between patronage and the arts that his company was both akin to and at pains to separate itself from. As Sharon O'Dair, following Louis Montrose, has shown, "On the one hand, *Dream* mocks or burlesques the efforts of the amateur thespians. This mockery is part of a strategy of professionalization, by which Shakespeare distinguishes 'the mechanicals' art from that of the Lord Chamberlain's Men'" (16). To what extent are the creators of our documentaries, or we as viewers, mirroring this early modern dynamic? To what extent are we flattered to be cast as overlords, even as we encourage these middling upstarts to become new men? In his essay on the pastoral, Montrose cites William Empson, who claimed that the "essential trick of the old pastoral, which was felt to imply a beautiful relation between rich and poor, was to make simple people express strong feelings . . . in learned and fashionable language" (417). This seems an apt description of Shakespeare's function in our documentaries, and it is also an apt description of the ideological mystification performed by underdog documentary. It's worth noting that Empson himself cites Grierson's *Drifters* (1929) as a documentary film that provides "a pastoral feeling" (8). Though the "wretchedness" depicted in our films is more often located in the inner city, the logic and structure of the pastoral still apply. Long after the postbellum great migrations of African-Americans to urban centers, and in the wake of white flight, we might consider how today's Shakespearean documentaries index the seemingly paradoxical idea of what I'd like to call "the inner-city pastoral." Montrose also cites Burke in order to describe the way in which the pastoral form, much like our films or the play within the play in *Dream*, "deals with 'class consciousness' not by emphasizing conflict but by aiming at 'a stylistic transcending of conflict' in symbols of communion, thereby contributing to the 'mystification of class'" (417). In the next section, I would like to more closely examine how these documentaries use Shakespeare to transcend conflict by "mak[ing] simple people express strong feelings . . . in learned and fashionable language." What's more, I would like to look at how such feelings infect audiences and, both on and off screen, are figured as therapeutic ends in themselves.

2 Pedagogy under Emotional Capitalism

In her examination of two of the films analyzed here, *The Hobart Shakespeareans* and *Why Shakespeare?*, Ayanna Thompson observes that discussions of race in these films are either conspicuously absent or raised only to be quickly disavowed (122). The same might be said for the way class works in nearly all of these films. While Sarah Olive has astutely argued that, in such Shakespeare documentaries, "Shakespeare is figured as the elusive thing to 'own' along with the likes of a thin body, unlined face, beautiful house, love of opera or pimped car touted elsewhere on reality television," I think Shakespeare's role goes beyond that of a status-enhancing commodity (7). Thompson contends, instead, that "Shakespeare symbolically stands in for a body politic that seeks both to accept and to digest/melt away the racial, ethnic, cultural, and social differences of those who may not at first glance appear to be part of the whole: Make Yourself American through Will Power" (130). The ideas of acceptance, assimilation, national consolidation, and integration are important here, but equally important is the way in which markers of class or race are effaced in the name of "the teleological move towards personal improvement" (122). It's useful to recall here Kahana's claim that documentary works allegorically, displacing the particular in the name of the abstract. If, as Claire Bishop claims, the most successful socially engaged participatory arts are those that best navigate the "dual horizon" and allow "specific instances to become generalizable, establishing *a relationship* between the particular and the universal," a problem arises when the universal displaces the particular (272; my emphasis). In her critique of participatory documentaries, Pooja Rangan describes how "the liberatory practice of claiming [participants'] humanity inevitably entails the abjection and exclusion of the particular, embodied facts of difference, which are seen as a primitive form of captivity" (6). Rangan goes on to discuss how "[t]he practice of othering . . . has also taken on supple new forms that operate not through exclusion and setting apart but through inclusion, participation, and empowerment" (6).

Many of the films examined here figure Shakespeare and performance as a means of accessing just such a "common humanity" or "shared national heritage," often at the expense of the particularity of or differences within their engaged communities. In *Why Shakespeare?* David St. John tells us that the "gift" of Shakespeare lies in how "Shakespeare teaches us what it means to be human." In many ways, this abstract humanity has long been the desired outcome of the arts and humanities programs in schools and at the national level. Bishop notes, "In the UK, New Labour (1997–2010) deployed a rhetoric almost identical to that of practitioners of socially engaged art in order to justify spending on the arts. Anxious for accountability, the question it asked on entering office in 1997 was: what can the arts do for society? The answers included increasing employability, minimising crime, [and] fostering aspiration" (13). Our documentaries seem to draw strikingly similar conclusions about the role of the arts, but Bishop's critique further explains Rangan's argument that othering might happen through inclusion and participation:

> The solution implied by the discourse of social exclusion is simply the goal of transition across the boundary from excluded to included, to allow people to access the holy grail of self-sufficient consumerism and be independent of any need for welfare. Furthermore, social exclusion is rarely perceived to be a corollary of neoliberal policies, but of any number of peripheral (and individual) developments, such as drug-taking, crime, family breakdown and teenage pregnancy. (13)

According to the logic employed by these films, in the United Kingdom and the United States, marginalized communities are composed of self-defeating, self-marginalizing, failed individuals or families who, through the power of the arts, might be better interpellated into healthy national cultures. And it seems that both Conservatives and Labour, Democrats and Republicans, have reached consensus on this logic.

The New Labour discourse of inclusion has its corollary in the United States and is best illustrated by two innovations spearheaded by the Bush administration: No Child Left Behind (NCLB) – the 2001 reauthorization of the Elementary and Secondary Education Act of 1965 (part of Johnson's War on Poverty) – and the NEA's populist project, Shakespeare in American Communities (SIAC). On October 28, 2003, Capitol Hill was abuzz with performances of Shakespeare. The night served as an inauguration and celebration of the NEA's new national program, what acting NEA chairman Dana Gioia, who was a Stanford MBA turned poet before Bush appointed him chairman of the NEA in 2003, called "the most ambitious program in the history of the NEA" ("Introduction for Teachers"). Gioia notes that it is the "largest government-sponsored theatrical program since the Federal Theatre Project of the WPA era" ("Chairman's Message" 1). "Phase Two," the pedagogical phase of the program, called Shakespeare for a New Generation (SNG), is an outreach program aiming to engage students in every state of the union. Shakespeare for a New Generation has two component parts: the NEA provides grants to local theater companies, allowing them to tour (and provide workshops at) local middle and high schools, and it also distributes a multimedia teacher's kit to teachers across the USA free of charge.

The multimedia kit includes two films, an audio CD, a teacher's guide, a series of posters and timelines of Shakespeare's life, and a collection of monologues students can use to engage in "recitation contests" (1). The NEA boasts that, through SNG, "more than 1.5 million people" were able to attend productions of Shakespeare's plays" ("About"). According to Arts Midwest, the NEA's partner, more than 4,400 communities have been visited by more than 111 companies; the program has hosted "45,000 related educational activities at more than 10,000 schools and juvenile justice [*sic*] facilities . . . in all 50 states." By 2008, Gioia could claim that 55,000 copies of the NEA's free multimedia kit had been requested and "have been used by more than 20 million students" (NEA "2008 Guide").

Why Shakespeare? is a short film funded and produced by the NEA. The DVD, not currently for sale, is the centerpiece of the SNG multimedia kit. The film addresses students directly and is narrated in large part by Dana Gioia. It features celebrities such as Tom Hanks, Michael Richards, William Shatner, and Martin Sheen, along with professors, actors, and students narrating their experiences with the "transformative" power of Shakespeare. Gioia reminisces, in the film, about the "incredible sort of transformative experience" he had connecting with art as a child. Mel Stuart's *The Hobart Shakespeareans* (2005) is a related, made-for-television PBS documentary that follows Los Angeles elementary school teacher Rafe Esquith as he uses Shakespeare and performance to teach a class composed entirely of non-native English speakers. In Germany, *The Hobart Shakespeareans* was released as *Shakespeare für Migrantenkinder*, "Shakespeare for Migrant Children." Esquith, who has also written four books on teaching, was awarded the NEA's National Medal of Arts by Bush. He was the first teacher in the history of the NEA to receive this award. He has also been commended by the queen of England, the Dalai Lama, Disney, Johns Hopkins, the Royal Shakespeare Company (RSC), and of course, Oprah Winfrey. Esquith was directly connected to SNG; the NEA established a "players guild" of "arts experts and actors," a group that included Esquith, along with Harold Bloom, Michael York, Julie Taymor, James Earl Jones, Jane Alexander, Michael Kahn, Angela Lansbury, and – somehow – Hilary Duff ("NEA Announces").

Under Bush's leadership, the conservative antipathy toward the NEA that calcified during the culture wars was suddenly reversed as Bush began increasing NEA funding during each year of his administration (NEA "Appropriations"). A similar reversal was inaugurated by Bush's NCLB legislation. Henry A. Giroux observes, "Unlike the Republican party agenda of the past, which called for the abolition of the U.S. Department of Education and a diminished federal presence in shaping educational policy, Bush has called for an expanded federal role in education along with increased funding" (72). These investments inevitably and radically reshaped the agencies they were ostensibly reforming, a transformation that continued with renewed fervor under Barack Obama's 2009 Race to the Top grant initiative, which further incentivized neoliberal reforms. Megan Erickson argues, "The connections NCLB established between standards-based reformers, education equity, and marketization was not only useful for political grandstanding, but also essential to the successful advancement of the neoliberal agenda – cost-cutting, union busting, the intensification of competition, and privatization – in American public schools" (94). The Shakespearean documentaries of the past two decades perfectly coincide with this wave of neoliberal "reform" within public education and public arts funding. I would like to explore, in what follows, how these films both register and champion the values and discourses associated with these reform movements. Because of the unique neoliberal transformations that occurred during the Bush administration, and because this period witnessed the emergence of a new genre of Shakespearean teaching documentaries, I give this period more attention than subsequent periods. Many, though by no means all, of the reform movements witnessed during the Bush administration peak and then begin to fade during the Obama administration. Under the Trump administration, we have witnessed a return to the Republican agenda to defund the NEA and a move away from federal regulatory programs like No Child Left Behind or Race to the Top. Attempts to defund the NEA have been successfully blocked for the time being; meanwhile, the Trump administration's NEA, through its Creative Forces: NEA Military Healing Arts Network initiative, has supported and emphasized the therapeutic potential of the arts to redress the effects of PTSD and traumatic brain injury in soldiers. I address this therapeutic turn, already a part of the NEA's agenda during the Bush administration, in the second half of this Element.

I want to now look more closely at an intersection between economics and education in *The Hobart Shakespeareans*. In the film, Rafe Esquith touts his "money system," a system that has been "emulated around the world." We get more insight on the matter in a lecture Esquith gave for the Lavin Agency. In the lecture, Esquith talks about how students in his class are interpellated into a capitalist ideology that naturalizes and valorizes the "principle of ownership" (Esquith). His comments are worth quoting at length:

> I wanted my kids to understand America, so I decided – I think you'll get a big kick out of this – our economic system. When children come into class . . . they have to apply for a job . . . The problem is, they have to pay rent to sit at their desks. The closer they sit to the front of the room, the higher the rent is; it's a better neighborhood. Now I'm so devious, that I do not pay them enough money to be able to make their rent at the end of the month. And if you cannot make your rent at the end of the month, you're evicted from your seat, and you have to sit on the floor as a homeless person; however, I give them thousands of opportunities to make extra money, by doing extra assignments, by working hard,

by doing good deeds, and by the end of the month, not only
can they pay their rent, [but] for the children who are really
frugal and conservative with their money, if you can save up
triple your rent, you can buy your seat, call it a condomi-
nium, and then you don't have to pay rent anymore, to teach
them the principle of ownership [applause], and the really
clever kids, the really clever kids, save their money, and buy
other kids' seats, and charge *them* rent every month.
(Esquith)

Esquith's money system has indeed been widely adopted. The Vanguard
Group, a financial services company, boasts that it provides its free "classroom management system," a similar money system, to educators in all fifty
states (My Classroom Economy). The program, however, made the news in
March 2019 when parents complained that their children were sitting on the
floor and unable to use the bathroom because they lacked school dollars
(Dornfield). Esquith's and Vanguard's models, nightmarish pedagogies
epitomizing those critiqued so thoroughly by the critical pedagogy movement in the last half of the twentieth century, mirror the rhythm and mode
of production of a particular form of capitalism. Classroom-as-workplace or
classroom-as-marketplace structural homologies were mainstays of many
twentieth-century critiques of schooling, most notably in the critiques of
Althusser, in which he asserts that the school is the "dominant ideological
state apparatus" (104), and in the work of Samuel Bowles and Herbert
Gintis. Reflecting recently on their landmark study *Schooling in Capitalist
America*, Bowles and Gintis remember their structuralist argument:
"Schools accomplish [socialization] by what we called the *correspondence
principle*, namely, by structuring social interactions and individual rewards
to replicate the environment of the workplace" (1). This classroom-work-
place metaphor, however, works differently in the post-Fordist economy of
late capitalism. In this model, as in Freire's *Pedagogy of the Oppressed*, the
dialectical struggle between the teacher's authority and the student's desire
for liberation corresponds to a larger dialectical class struggle as it appears
in the workplace. Freire sought an alternative to what he saw as the
"banking concept" of education, a dialectical opposition between

authoritative teachers and passively receptive students, a system wherein "knowledge is a gift bestowed by those who consider themselves knowledgeable upon those whom they consider to know nothing" (53). Today, however, this banking concept, wherein passive students "have the illusion of acting through the action of the teacher," cannot begin to account for the capitalist logic of Esquith's classroom, a room in which students are often actively moving, performing, playing music, and engaging with each other (54).

As Claire Bishop and others have noted, the pedagogical revolutions of the 1960s coincided with aesthetic revolutions in theater. This is perhaps most legible in the connection between Augusto Boal's *Theatre of the Oppressed* and Freire's *Pedagogy of the Oppressed*, but we could just as easily locate homologies between Brechtian aesthetics and Giroux's critical pedagogy. In 2012, Bishop asks an important question about this interdisciplinary inheritance: "But if both critical pedagogy and participatory arts effectively produce a form of institutional critique within their respective disciplines in the 1960s, what does it mean for these two modes to converge so frequently today, as they do in the projects of the past decade?" (267). The participatory dynamics of the classrooms depicted in the pedagogical and performance-based documentaries of the twenty-first century seem poised to challenge the hierarchies upset by radical theater and pedagogy. However, Nicholson argues, "The emphasis on marginality in applied theatre has not, by and large, taken account of the potential slippage of liminality into conservatism, nor how quickly theatre practices and pedagogies once regarded as 'alternative' become absorbed into the mainstream" (53). She locates evidence of such slippage by observing a similar erosion between the discourses of performance studies and those of "performance management": "Despite different motives and intentions, aspects of performance management have crept into the kinds of organizations on which applied theatre depends for its funding – such as charities, educational institutions, hospitals, prisons and voluntary organisations," all of whom want to instrumentalize performance and measure its ability to achieve these institutions' targets, indicators, and outcomes (56–57).

As both Bishop and Nicholson note, the strongest and most persuasive contemporary critique of Marxian pedagogies and theater practices comes from Jacques Rancière, who, in his book *The Emancipated Spectator*, uses

Joseph Jacotot's conceptualization of "the ignorant schoolmaster" to question the very hierarchies and distances both critical pedagogy and radical theater work to combat. Rancière locates "the first conviction that theatrical reformers share with stultifying pedagogues: that of a gulf separating two positions" through which knowledge must pass, a gulf between passivity and activity, a gulf between alienation and freedom (11–12). He asks, "But could we not invert the terms of the problem by asking if it is not precisely this desire to abolish the distance that creates it?" (12). It seems to me that Rancière's reversal mirrors the logic of Adorno's critique, when the latter asks if our attachment to underdog narratives arises from our investments in a culture that presupposes the naturalness of the capitalist classifications of winner and underdog. If we assume the hierarchies and gulfs questioned by Rancière, and if we assume the naturalness of an underclass, we have no choice but to imagine the aims of progressive pedagogy or theater within what Bishop calls "the social inclusion agenda," whose "mission is to enable all members of a society to be self-administering fully functioning consumers who do not rely on the welfare state and who can cope with a deregulated, privatised world" (14). Rancière does much to reframe the oppositions that subtend radical theater's and critical pedagogy's historical projects:

> [I]t is the network of presuppositions, the set of equivalences between theatrical audience and community, gaze and passivity, exteriority and separation, mediation and simulacrum; oppositions between the collective and the individual, the image and living reality, activity and passivity, self-ownership and alienation. This set of equivalences and oppositions in fact composes a rather intricate dramaturgy of sin and redemption. (7)

There is no redemption without sin, and when our documentaries deploy a rhetoric of redemption they cannot do so without assuming, first, the sin of their participants. The ignorant schoolmaster, on the other hand, makes no assumptions about the gulf separating teacher from student. Students need not be redeemed.

In *The Hobart Shakespeareans*, as in so many of these films, Shakespeare stands as a figure of bourgeois refinement, the "learned and refined language" through which "simple people" are redeemed as they bridge the gulf between their ignorant pasts and their enlightened futures as bourgeois consumers of culture. Beyond this, I hope to show how these films, on the one hand, figure a mastery of Shakespearean performance as a means of access to both self-mastery and self-discovery; however, on the other hand, this mastery and discovery of the emotions – and the emotional labor such mastery and discovery entail – ultimately bypasses the self in order to produce the modes of comportment required by the bourgeois workplace. In *Kings of Baxter*, Huw McKinnon of Bell Shakespeare says of his incarcerated teen actors: "If they're a bit more confident in that job interview, or a bit more confident getting that rental property a few years down the track, then this program has had its intended effect." While confidence is perhaps not likely to factor significantly into one's ability to rent an apartment (as opposed to, say, credit history or income), McKinnon's comments index how self-improvement's ultimate telos is bourgeois inclusion.

In many of these documentaries, performance is also positioned as a radical alternative to other forms of learning, which are, by contrast, imagined as dull, asocial, alienating, and emotionally lifeless. In *Why Shakespeare?* Gioia stresses how the arts cater to those on the margins, noting that "not all kids are good at what you think of as conventional schoolwork." But it remains important to ask: how might these films index the ways in which alternative pedagogies and applied theater practices of the late twentieth century have been recuperated by new forms of capitalism? Nicholson highlights one of the important ways in which such a recuperation might happen. She writes, in the spirit of Rancière's critique, that "the assumption that active, collective participation is necessarily oppositional to capitalism has been subject to scrutiny in the twenty-first century. There is, of course, no guarantee that collaborative process-based art-making is inherently radical, particularly in an era of increased affective audience participation in everything from TV talent shows to immersive performances in old cellars" (13). In what follows, I would like to look at how a number of these documentaries deploy "increased affective [student] participation" in the service of neoliberal capital.

The language and performance of emotion suffuse the classroom in *The Hobart Shakespeareans*. Students are expected to weep and express their joy

Figure 2 Emotional labor in *The Hobart Shakespeareans* (2005)

or gratitude, and as much as they learn to sell their emotions on stage, they learn that it's even more important to give the emotional hard sell when they're off stage yet under the anthropological gaze of the documentary camera's lens (see Figures 2 and 3). As Nicholson admits, "when I read that participants have expressed profound changes in attitude I often wonder whether they have been complicit in following the 'script' of the workshop, or whether their change of heart indicates a positive but temporary identification with a kindly practitioner whose point of view may not be actually expressed, but whose values are nonetheless clearly visible to them" (83). Sarah Olive is similarly skeptical about the way such films frame the emotionally transformative power of Shakespeare, noting that "any change [in students] might be more demonstrably attributed to drama methods, school excursions and the experience of being filmed *per se*" (7). Students raised in the era of reality television know too well how such confessions

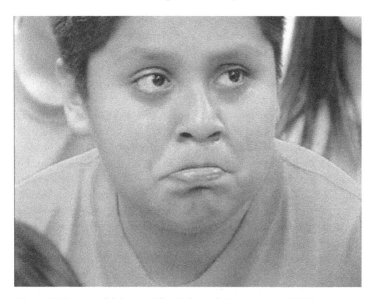

Figure 3 Emotional labor in The Hobart Shakespeareans (2005)

and testimonials conventionally work. Mark Fisher draws a significant comparison between changing workplace attitudes and the affective register of reality television. "What we are forced into is not merely work, in the old sense of undertaking an activity we don't want to perform; no, now we are forced to act as if we want to work. Even if we want to work in a burger franchise, we have to prove that, like reality TV contestants, *we really want it*" ("Suffering" 536).

In his review of *The Hobart Shakespeareans*, Rory L. Aronsky comments that "the students become emotional over the words. Actually emotional!" In the film, Sir Ian McKellen enters Hobart Elementary and exclaims, "I don't know why, but every time I'm in this room I feel like crying!" We also see this connection between Shakespeare's language and the "heart" in *Why Shakespeare?* Ben Donenberg, the artistic director for the LA Shakespeare Festival, highlights what he sees as the affective power of Shakespeare's meter: "Da-DUM. Shakespeare's telling you or sharing or reflecting the heartbeat of his characters and asking your heart to synch up with theirs; that's all iambic pentameter is." Interestingly, Donenberg directed the production of *Henry V* to which Mr. Rago takes his recruits in *Renaissance Man* (Shirley 46).

Romeo Is Bleeding (2015) follows Donté Clark, a twenty-two-year-old black man from North Richmond, CA, an area notorious for crime, as he works on an "autobiographical adaptation of *Romeo and Juliet*," a version in which he aims to "take a Shakespeare play, rewrite it, and make it fit Richmond." This adaptation is titled *Té's Harmony* (Té and Harmony substitute for Romeo and Juliet, respectively). It's worth noting that this film appears uncharacteristic of its genre in three respects. First, for the most part, those doing the teaching and creating are black Richmond residents, not outsiders or professionals. However, neither Clark's teacher and mentor, Molly Raynor, who is also the cousin of the film's director, Jason Zeldes, nor Rooben Morgan, the director of *Té's Harmony*, are Richmond natives. It's also important to note that, while the film champions harmony and peace within the largely black communities of Central and North Richmond, the infrastructure that supports such change is Breaking Waves, a charter school founded by John H. Scully, founder of SPO Partners, a private investment company and merchant bank, and Pastor Eugene Farlough. However, unlike in all of the other films examined here, the students significantly rework Shakespeare's text. Whereas nearly all of these films require students to assimilate to Shakespeare, this film assimilates Shakespeare to a very specific context. Ayanna Thompson advises, in her study of "reform Shakespeare" programs, that "[r]eform programs that utilize Shakespeare, thus, should look to reform Shakespeare," and the film accomplishes this much very well (143). Third, this film, more than any other, glances at the region's larger history and social context. Throughout the film, however, the problem of urban violence is nevertheless frequently reduced to skirmishes between individuals. We are told, by residents and police officers, that the violent decades-long feud between North and Central Richmond originated in a dispute between two motorists, and it is suggested that this incident accounts for the region's subsequent violence and incarceration. As with so many allegories of *Romeo and Juliet*, once the play's "feud" is removed from the feudalism of its context, we have no need to look for systemic motivations for violence. That said, the curricular materials sold on the film's website do a much better job contextualizing the city's violence than the film itself.

Emotional and performance management are central to this film's mission. At a meeting in which the project's managers discuss the project's participants, Raynor assesses D'Neise Robinson's performance as Harmony: "But at the end of the day, their well-being affects everything else, you know, their emotional well-being, and I think that with D'Neise, she's so tough that she doesn't want to make herself vulnerable. She thinks that it's weak to cry, that it's weak to be soft." Raynor stresses the need for Robinson to "break down and be soft and be vulnerable and be tough and be Richmond at the same time." While Raynor's insight regarding how one might need to "be Richmond" does situate emotional economies within material contexts, in these comments, Raynor echoes many of the teachers of such youth when she stresses the need for tears, for softness, for vulnerability. The argument here, that marginalized and precarious youth do not know how to be vulnerable, is paradoxical at best, harmful at worst. When Clark visits the Alameda County Juvenile Justice Center to perform his spoken word poetry (a poetry with historical bite and political acumen less salient in the group's Shakespearean adaptation), a correctional officer tells him of the emotional effect he had on one inmate: "You have a connection with him. I've never seen an emotion out of him, and he be comin' here for a while. All of this emotion came out when he was talkin' to you, all of it."

In *My Shakespeare: Romeo for a New Generation with Baz Luhrmann*, a British film with a structure not unlike *Romeo Is Bleeding*, in the sense that a black local artist works with members of his own community under the mentorship of a white professional, veteran actor Patterson Joseph becomes frustrated with the perceived lack of emotion produced by his cast. He asks, "Shall I tell you what we're going to do? Yeah, I will. It's basically an hour and a half of an emotional workshop. Okay? You're gonna come, you're gonna weep, you're gonna shout, you're gonna laugh, you're gonna cry, everything." The film's narrator tells us in voiceover that the emotional workshop will help "actors unlock real and powerful feelings." Jonathan Taylor, the actor playing Romeo, replies, "We's all like, [shocked expression] 'Hang on, this is Harlesdon; this is the ghetto. We don't have emotions in the ghetto." Joseph, at one point, acknowledges the situatedness of emotion, when he comments on his cast's fear of emotion: "I don't know whether it's just their lifestyle, their world. 'Don't show too much joy because it might come down.' You don't hope too much because it might all turn to shit. When your world picture is 'got to be cool,' 'mustn't expose yourself,' 'mustn't look like an idiot,' it's very hard." Sara Ahmed reminds us, however, of the way in which hardness is often figured as a lack of emotion, whereas "[*h*]*ardness is not the absence of emotion, but a different emotional orientation towards others*," one that is perhaps justified given these young performers' situation (4). Joseph reminds his cast, "Don't get angry; there are other emotions to play." What is, ostensibly, an exercise in "bringing out" emotions, what Ahmed calls the psychologically inflected "'inside-out' model of emotions" – a model in which emotions are figured as private, interior properties – ends up being, in fact, an attempt to mold and shape emotion (9).

Near the end of *Shakespeare High*, a film directed by Alex Rotaru (who was the principal cinematographer, editor, and coproducer on *The Hobart Shakespeareans*), we hear a testimonial from Tosh Alexander Hall, a student from PUC Charter who used to be a bully and "a little bit thug-like." He testifies, after winning the regional performance competition for his role as Bottom: "I'm blessed to have theater because without that I have nothing. Theater's the only thing that made me have tears of joy." We then linger on a freeze-frame of him weeping. While these eruptions of feeling might seem like private, individual affairs, psychological rather than sociological events, in fact, emotion now lies at the heart of academic, artistic, and market labor. As Ahmed advises, we must attend to "the very public nature of emotions, and the emotive nature of publics (14). Arlie Russell Hochschild first explored the relationship between private emotions and public commerce, what she termed "emotional labor," in her 1983 book *The Managed Heart: Commercialization of Human Feeling* (7). There, she details the way in which internalized guides for feeling establish "feeling rules," rules that lay out the framework for an "emotional gift exchange" in both public and private settings (56, 84). In describing such feeling rules, Hochschild borrows the language of the theater: "Rules as to the type, intensity, duration, timing, and placing of feelings are society's guidelines, the promptings of an unseen director. The stage, the props, and fellow members of the cast help us internally assemble the gifts that we freely exchange" (85). She also notes that "[c]ompanies, prisons, schools, churches – institutions of virtually any sort – assume some of the functions of a director and alter the relation of actor to director" (49).

In describing the emotional dramaturgy of everyday life, Hochschild builds upon the work of Erving Goffman, who first wed performance studies to sociology, showing how "life itself is a dramatically enacted thing. All the world is not, of course, a stage, but the crucial ways in which it isn't are not easy to specify" (72). Goffman was also concerned with the way in which social structures shape human emotion, and his project is in many ways already committed to illustrating what he terms "a certain bureaucratization of the spirit" (56). Hochschild's concept of "emotional labor" is now a cultural commonplace, appearing everywhere, from *The Guardian* to *Forbes*. Hochschild is credited with showing the way in which emotional labor is gendered, but she does more than this. Like Goffman, who was also interested in the gendered nature of social performance, Hochschild is attentive to more than the gendering of emotional labor. She writes, "On the whole, I would guess that women, Protestants, and middle-class people cultivate the habit of suppressing their own feeling more than men, Catholics, and lower-class people do . . . the very ways in which we acknowledge feeling rules reflect where we stand on the social landscape" (57). Nearly absent from her study is a consideration of how race might complicate this picture of gender, religion, and class.

In her studies of what she terms "emotional capitalism," sociologist Eva Illouz complicates Hochschild's thesis, arguing that the gendered nature of emotional management in the workplace had already begun to shift when industrial psychologists like Elton Mayo, in the late 1920s, produced studies that eventually "transposed women's emotional culture to the workplace and legitimized it" (*Saving* 77). Labor history shows us that capital in the twentieth century transformed, from its roots in manufacturing and material production, to a new stage where, under late capitalism, immaterial labor – customer service, care work, and communications – dominate, changing the very nature of work and how we might imagine vocational education. In her trilogy of related books, *Cold Intimacies: The Making of Emotional Capitalism*, *Saving the Modern Soul: Therapy, Emotions, and the Culture of*

Self-Help, and *Oprah Winfrey and the Clamour of Misery: An Essay on Popular Culture*, Illouz shows how the self-help industry, therapeutic discourses, daytime talk shows like the *Oprah Winfrey Show*, and concepts like "emotional intelligence" have worked in lockstep with business communities and public relations departments throughout the twentieth century, with the effect that "[e]motional capitalism realigned emotional cultures, making the economic self emotional and emotions more closely harnessed to instrumental action" (*Cold Intimacies* 23). Illouz frames this realignment as a merging of *homo oeconomicus* and *homo sentimentalis*.

It is within this context that these Shakespearean documentaries train their sights on student emotion, showcasing performance pedagogies' ability to produce emotional discipline and transformation. These documentaries, and the larger reality television genre, when they employ therapeutic discourses rooted in emotional management, displace sociological analysis with individualized psychological scrutiny, largely in the name of increasing student competence. Illouz's study shows how psychology similarly mystified and subdued class conflict in the early twentieth-century workplace: "Psychologists seemed to promise that they would increase profits, fight labor unrest, organize manager-worker relationships in a nonconfrontational way, and neutralize class struggle by casting them in the benign language of emotion and personality" (*Saving* 86–87). The films examined here continue this tradition of couching social antagonisms in the "benign language of emotion and personality." In her book *Feeling Power: Emotions and Education*, Megan Boler argues that, despite Mayo's attempts to emotionalize the workplace, his psychological models did not completely replace Taylorism: "By the middle of [the twentieth] century, industrial psychologists were favoring Mayo's approach over Taylor's. However, scientific management was by no means abandoned: The manipulation of human resources was simply combined with efficiency models" (67). This layering of modes of production – material and affective – is mirrored in Rafe Esquith's classroom, where his "money system" is supplemented by the emotional labor required of student performance.

But Esquith's classroom is far from the only one adopting such models. Boler and Illouz have studied the influence of conceptions of "emotional intelligence" in the classroom and the workplace, respectively, since Daniel

Goleman coined the term in his 1995 book *Emotional Intelligence: Why It Can Matter More than IQ*. Goleman's book became a sensation and contributes to the shape and tenor of the therapeutic discourses on display on *The Oprah Winfrey Show* (Illouz, *Oprah Winfrey* 164). Illouz compares the notion of cultural capital, "the capacity to relate to cultural artifacts in a way that signals familiarity with high culture sanctioned by the upper classes," to the way in which psychologists "contributed to making emotional style a social currency – capital – but also articulated a new language of selfhood to seize that capital" (*Cold Intimacies* 64). This therapeutic self, with its EQ and IQ, finds a training ground in the affective dimensions of the K–12 classroom. Boler, who surveyed and analyzed a host of "emotional literacy curricula," concludes that, "despite the apparent interest in social relations . . . [b]oth as a management strategy, and as a curriculum that can teach students to manage conflict and delay gratification, emotional intelligence casts the social self in entirely individualistic terms," making it a "neoliberal variation of genetic discourses regarding intelligence" (e.g., the mental hygiene movement of the early twentieth century) (63, 64–65).

In the next section, I would like to further explore the way in which our films register the new contours of emotional capitalism, paying particular attention to the self-help logic informing the new initiatives and political paradigms that dominate discussions of education and welfare reform.

3 Self-Help Culture and the New Paternalism

The youth depicted in these films are not the only ones laboring emotionally; their first audiences, those who aim to teach participants to feel properly, are also overcome by emotion. What's more, in this way, as the second audience, we receive cues for how to feel. *Why Shakespeare?* features a scene in which Dana Gioia recalls a performance of Henry's Saint Crispin's Day speech given by one of the students from Hobart Elementary at the inauguration of SIAC:

> Now this little boy had been raised in a non-English-speaking home. And as he built this magnificent speech towards its climax, I found myself weeping, and I was terribly

embarrassed by this, but I noticed finally when it was over –
all this was in the US Capitol – I looked around the room,
and everyone else was crying too.

What is going on in this scene? How does this elementary school student's
performance produce such emotion? What prompts Gioia to give this student
a world of sighs? Documentary filmmaker Adam Curtis offers this insight:
"TV now tells you what to feel. It doesn't tell you what to think any more.
From EastEnders to reality format shows, you're on the emotional journey of
people – and through the editing, it gently suggests to you what is the agreed
form of feeling. 'Hugs and Kisses,' I call it ... It really is a system not of
moral guidance, but of emotional guidance" (qtd. in Fisher, *Capitalist Realism*
74). I hope to show in the remaining sections how the applied theater depicted
in these films – and the films themselves – works by providing emotional *and*
moral guidance to discipline their participants and viewers regarding how to
feel and live properly. Additionally, I hope to illustrate Shakespeare's role in
providing such "hugs and kisses" moments, what Cole calls the "big emotional experiences that validate privilege." But before we can explore how
emotional capitalism disciplines our emotions, we must first examine the rise
of twentieth- and twenty-first-century self-help discourses and the surprising
role Prince Hal plays therein.

Eva Illouz has traced therapeutic self-help discourses from the rags-to-
riches narratives of the nineteenth century, which were written for entrepreneurial men (e.g., Samuel Smiles's 1859 *Self-Help*), into the 1930s, when the
paperback revolution made the consumption of such literature affordable,
widespread, and addressed to a broader audience, to the 1950s and 1960s,
when, as a result of the 1946 National Mental Health Act, "psychology expand
[ed] the scope of its influence to the 'normally' neurotic middle-class people"
(*Cold Intimacies* 40, 43, 25). By mid-century, "the state increasingly used
therapy in many of the services it offered, such as social work, prison
rehabilitation, education, and the courts," many of the same institutional
sites where we find Shakespeare being put to work (58). By the end of the
century, therapeutic self-help discourses had become the dominant framework through which to imagine social and individual provision. Social
welfare had been reimagined as individual well-being. Micki McGee, in her

Self-Help, Inc.: Makeover Culture in America, describes how, alongside the growth of neoliberalism's austerity policies and the widening of the gap between rich and poor, "[b]etween 1972 and 2000 the number of self-help books more than doubled" (11). During the period just prior to the emergence of our Shakespearean documentaries, between 1991 and 1996, "self-help book sales rose 96 percent," a phenomenon that explains why so many Americans came to believe "that self-fulfillment might serve as a genuine sign of one's secular salvation" (11, 111). As we have seen, these documentaries, in general, eschew social analysis and instead focus on private, individual, emotional, familial, and psychological solutions to more systemic problems. Self-help literature popularizes and naturalizes a similar discourse. What's more, this self-help ethos proliferates at just the historical moment in which systemic social problems were finally beginning to be addressed as such, effectively recuperating the energy of many more radical countercultural discourses of self-fulfillment (feminism and civil rights movements, for example) (112). More recently, the 2020 Democratic presidential primaries boosted the visibility of Marianne Williamson, a new-age self-help author of thirteen books and a spiritual advisor to Oprah Winfrey. Though she ended her presidential bid in early 2020, the motivational and spiritual ethos of her campaign attracted much attention. The *New York Times* framed the contest between Williamson and Donald Trump as "the motivational guru versus the reality TV president" (Kestenbaum). These two discourses – self-help and reality television – play a key role in shaping and framing contemporary Shakespearean documentaries, but they also have enough ballast to frame a presidential contest.

If, as McGee argues, "within the cultures of self-improvement, values from the competitive world of the marketplace have been transplanted to the personal world of intimate life, and vice-versa," as in emotional capitalism, no wonder then that we find, within the age of reform inaugurated by NCLB, a national pedagogical and curricular movement founded on similar values, one that deploys Shakespeare in the name of such entrepreneurial values. The curricula of our documentaries, unsurprisingly, follow the model of programs using Shakespeare's plays to motivate, inspire, and instruct executives, programs such as the Movers & Shakespeares program run by former Reagan advisor and former chairman and CEO of Lockheed Martin, Kenneth Adelman. Such programs isolate – and decontextualize – key decisions and moments of leadership exhibited by Shakespeare's characters – Henry V at the Battle of Agincourt is a perennial favorite – and use the plays as a corporate-management manual.[5] Megan Erickson argues that such entrepreneurial conceits now dominate K–12 education in the United States as it borrows more and more of its rationale (and funding) from the world of business:

> The management guru's vision of empowerment as a personal struggle, the CEO's conviction that individual success is limited only by a lack of ambition, life as a series of goals waiting to be met. The type of advice once reserved for dieters, rookie sales associates, and the unemployed is now repeated to public school children with new age fervor: Think positive. Set goals and achieve them. Reach for the stars. Race to the top. It's never too early to network. Just smile. (97)

Entrepreneurial self-help rhetoric infuses many aspects of Esquith's classroom in *The Hobart Shakespeareans*. His students all wear t-shirts upon which Shakespeare's portrait is punningly captioned with the perennial self-help slogan: "Will Power!" We see, posted prominently in his classroom, Esquith's twin mottos, pedagogical slogans that sound more like corporate missions and that are repeated throughout the film: "There are no shortcuts." "Be nice. Work hard." Such mottos wed the productive efficiency of Taylorism to the emotional contours of late capitalism. Esquith remarks on his mottos and his classroom culture:

> Once they're in a culture of excellence, I don't care what color they are – they do fine. You talk about political correctness – I mean, we actually have classes now like "How to teach Latino kids mathematics" or "How to

[5] For more on Shakespeare providing a "corporate-management manual," see Lanier, "Shakescorp Noir," Newstok (Newstrom), "Right," and Thompson, *Passing Strange*.

teach Asian children" and this – you know, two and two is
still four. We're making it so complicated . . . I don't care
what your background is, [if] you remember those things
[Be nice. Work hard.], you're going to do fine.

Through the repression of difference comes a unified and homogenous
"culture of excellence." Esquith defines this "culture of excellence" as "a
culture where people are good to each other, where hard work matters, and
character matters even more." In *The University in Ruins*, his study of the
corporatization of the university, Bill Readings devotes a chapter to such
empty appeals to excellence, arguing that "[e]xellence is thus the integrating
principle that allows for 'diversity' . . . to be tolerated without threatening
the unity of the system . . . And once excellence has been generally accepted
as an organizing principle, there is no need to argue about differing
definitions" (32–33). After working with Esquith for a year, Mike
Feinberg and David Levin borrowed his slogans and formed their
Knowledge Is Power Program (KIPP), the largest network of "nonprofit"
charter schools (or educational management organizations [EMOs]) in the
country (KIPP schools have an enrollment of 90,000 students in 209 schools
in 20 states) (Strauss).[6] Knowledge Is Power is also the "largest network of
paternalistic schools" (discussed later in this Element) (Whitman, *Sweating*
xv). It's important to note that the line between "nonprofit" and for-profit
charter schools is often one marking "a distinction without a difference," as
many of the companies attached to and working with ostensible nonprofits
(e.g., proprietary curriculum delivery systems, charter management organizations [CMOs], or real estate developers) often reap massive financial

---

[6] It's worth noting, in more than a footnote perhaps, that both Esquith and Feinberg
have recently been dismissed for alleged sexual misconduct (accusations against
Esquith included physical abuse and mismanagement of funds). Coincidentally,
perhaps, Kevin Spacey, who now faces accusations of sexually assaulting minors,
serves as the executive producer and de facto host and narrator of *Shakespeare
High*. For more on accusations against Feinberg and Esquith, see Hartocollis,
"Michael Feinberg," Torres and Blume, "Rafe Esquith Fired," and Blume, "L.A.
Unified Settles Lawsuits."

rewards, and often these for-profit companies are owned by the same people as the "nonprofit" charter school (Greene, "How to Profit"). Peter Greene reports in *Forbes* that the Department of Education has lost "roughly $1 billion" to charter waste and fraud ("Report").

Many of the films under consideration here reflect trends in the so-called educational reform movement of the 2000s, a movement that, along with NCLB and Race to the Top, pushed for: the expansion of charter schools, school choice, high-stakes testing and accountability, connecting teacher pay to student test scores, and drastic consequences for schools unable to meet mandated targets. The movement stressed limiting or bypassing the power of unions, offered technological solutions to pedagogical problems, and encouraged market solutions that would open up public schools to innovations provided by philanthropic donors and tech CEOs. After 2001, Diane Ravitch claims, the United States witnessed "the largest expansion in the history of philanthropic effort focused on public education" (199). She writes, "Unlike dissident school reform movements of the past, this one had the support of the nation's wealthiest foundations, corporate executives, Wall Street hedge fund managers, leaders of the technological sector, and the top elected officials of both major parties" (249). Ravitch tracks how, during the reform movement, which many joked might as well be called NCLB, "no consultant left behind," "[e]ducation entrepreneurship became an emerging growth industry" (246). This reform movement, which began during the Bush administration, continued with vehemence under Arne Duncan, Barack Obama's secretary of education (2009–2015), creating a neoliberal, bipartisan consensus around education that recent nationwide teachers' strikes are only now beginning to challenge. Obama perhaps chose Arne Duncan for the work he did as CEO of Chicago's public schools (2001–2009). The blueprint for his 2004 Renaissance 2010 initiative in Chicago implemented "a strategy for schools to more closely align with the goals of the business elite. Central to that strategy was the creation of 100 new charter schools, managed by for-profit businesses and freed of the city's local school councils and teacher's union – groups that have histori-cally put the welfare of the poor and minority students before that of the business sector" (Kumashiro). Duncan, as secretary of education, brought this reformist agenda to the national stage. But whereas Ravitch sees these new reforms as unprecedented, Erickson sees them as a return to the charity schools of the nineteenth century, which were "dependent on and shaped ideologically by the inclinations of the rich white donors obsessed with moral instruction of the poor rather than with providing universally high-quality education" (84).

It's no wonder, then, that this movement's aims and arguments were celebrated in the 2010 documentary *Waiting for Superman*, a film whose publicity was financed in part by Bill Gates ($2 million), who himself has given more than $100 million to CMOs (Ravitch 251, 210). The film, which was featured twice on the *Oprah Winfrey Show*, works like many of our Shakespearean documentaries. It follows marginalized youth as they attempt to attain coveted spots in charter schools. The film chronicles the desperate attempts of various marginalized youth and their families to move from underdog to middle-class respectability, but in lieu of a final performance, the film ends with the results of a public lottery, one that only a few students win. After a scene filled with children's and parents' tears, we learn that Anthony, a young black student hoping to attend the SEED charter and boarding school, though fifth on the waitlist, has been accepted. We follow him to his new dorm, as he lies on his new bed looking at a photo of his dead father. *Waiting for Superman* might be understood as a sequel to its equally successful predecessor *Hoop Dreams*, which, in 1994 laid the groundwork for how contemporary documentary might serve to critique public schools in the name of marginalized youth of color. Many of the schools featured in *Shakespeare High* are charter schools, as is the school featured in *Romeo Is Bleeding*. *The Hobart Shakespeareans* attend Hobart Elementary, a public school, but their endeavors are generously supported by a nonprofit organization founded by a former student, with additional support provided by "patrons." It's important to note that the historical scope of these films coincides with a massive growth of charter networks and EMOs. The authors of a recent report show that enrollment in for-profit EMOs jumped from 1,000 in 1996 to 462,926 in 2012 (Miron and Gulosino ii). It was estimated that by 2015, "EMO-operated schools enroll[ed] over 1.2 million students" (Baker and Miron 8).

Many of these films, *The Hobart Shakespeareans*, *Ballet Changed My Life*, *Fame High*, and *My Shakespeare* in particular, deploy an emergent, ostensibly reformist educational discourse belonging to what its proponents call "no-excuses schools" or "paternalistic schools." Arne Duncan's chief speechwriter, David Whitman, is a driving force behind the "new paternalism" in education. The title of the book in which he lays out his program, *Sweating the Small Stuff: Inner-City Schools and the New Paternalism*, signals his indebtedness to the literatures of self-help as it echoes (and inverts) the title of Richard Carlson's 1991 number one *New York Times* self-help bestseller, *Don't Sweat the Small Stuff and It's All Small Stuff: Simple Ways to Keep the Little Things from Taking Over*. Continuing in this vein, one of Whitman's key chapters lays out what he calls "the 20 habits of highly effective schools," a play on Stephen Covey's *The Seven Habits of Highly Effective People*, a 1989 international bestseller (*Sweating* 281). Among the habits Whitman lists are: "Eliminate (or at least disempower) local teacher unions"; "Tell students exactly how to behave and tolerate no disorder"; "Reject the culture of the streets" (displacing the particular in the name of an abstract culture of excellence); and "Give principals and teachers more autonomy – think 'charter school'" (259).

It is impossible to understand Whitman's reformist agenda without situating it within the larger framework of the new paternalism or what Paul Starobin has called "the Daddy State": "The purpose of government intervention is no longer to provide a safety net, as it was for the Nanny State, but to curtail bad behavior. Government acts not as a compliant supplier of personal needs, but as a demanding, if caring, enforcer of civic responsibilities. Nanny Staters are interested in social justice; Daddy Staters, in public order" (678). The logic of the "new paternalism" has its roots in Lawrence Mead's policy work, as explored in his 1997 *The New Paternalism: Supervisory Approaches to Poverty*. Mead, importantly, served as the architect of Bill Clinton's Personal Responsibility and Work Opportunity Reconciliation Act of 1996 (PRWORA), what Clinton memorably promised to be "the end of welfare as we know it." The new paternalism in the sphere of education is intricately linked to this landmark legislation, as well as other related and concomitant programs, from responsible fatherhood programs to abstinence and pregnancy prevention programs.

When Mead claims to be a "big government conservative" – one of the ways in which he separates himself from the violent legacy of older forms of paternalism, from slavery to Native American boarding schools – we might imagine this to be at odds with the aims of both neoconservativism and neoliberalism (Starobin 680). While "neoliberal paternalism" might seem like a contradiction in terms, because neoliberalism normally indexes a formation in which the state and its regulatory forces recede in order to make room for private market actors, in fact, "rather than limiting the state, neoliberalism envisions the state as a site for the application of market principles ... Through privatization and collaboration, they make the state more reliant on market actors to achieve public purposes" (Soss, Fording, and Schram 21). This bait-and-switch scheme mirrors how state-funded "nonprofit" CMOs organize and collaborate within a larger nexus of profit. Loïc Wacquant astutely reminds us how "'[s]mall government' in the economic register thus begets 'big government' on the twofold frontage of workfare and criminal justice" (308). We can add education to this twofold frontage. Elizabeth Ben-Ishai stresses, contrary to Mead's pro-government rhetoric, "the increasingly privatized nature of new paternalist programs, which often outsource elements of service delivery to nongovernmental organizations" (155). We witness such profitable outsourcing in a number of ersatz public spaces, from prisons to social programs to charter schools.

Such reforms market themselves as forward thinking or progressive, but the reorganizations of the social they perform are in fact deeply regressive. Laura Morgan notes how Clinton's welfare reform bill, the PRWORA, served as "the modern incarnation of the Elizabethan Poor Law," in that it aims to shift the responsibility for poverty onto individuals and families (qtd. in Cooper 105). Melinda Cooper, in her book *Family Values: Between Neoliberalism and the New Social Conservatism*, shows how, in an effort to repeal the broad social services introduced by the New Deal and Great Society, conservatives and the New Democrats aimed to return the United States to modes of social provision rooted in the 1601 Elizabethan Act of Relief of the Poor, which was "not only imported intact from England but [was] subsequently reinvented many times over" in order to tighten the link between familial and workplace responsibilities (73). Cooper tells us that "[i]n the late nineteenth century, the reinvigoration of the poor laws was aided and abetted by a new and flourishing enterprise of private charity, which supplemented the punitive power of the state with an intimate form of regulatory control extending into the homes of the urban poor" (84). We learn that in the 1960s, much of this poor law tradition was struck down in the courts, but beginning in the 1980s, "Reagan's welfare reform agenda sought to revive and extend a much older poor-law tradition of public relief, with its attendant *distinction between the deserving and the undeserving poor*" (99; my emphasis). As the new paternalism seeks, in the name of social welfare, to return us to nineteenth-century forms of social provision, the new Shakespearean documentary, too, deploys the forces of private charity to regulate a contest wherein we might make distinctions between the deserving and the undeserving poor.

Clinton took us even further into the nineteenth century than Reagan was able, even though his welfare bill was, importantly, first sketched out by Reagan (Cooper 106). Wacquant calls the PRWORA "one of the most regressive social programs promulgated by a democratic government in the twentieth century," one that "confirmed and accelerated the gradual replacement of a protective (semi-)welfare state by a disciplinary state mating the stinging goad of workfare with the dull hammer of prisonfare, for which the close monitoring and the punitive containment of derelict categories stand in for social policy toward the dispossessed" (79). But the rise of the prison industrial complex and the shift from welfare to workfare are not two separate innovations; for Wacquant, the specter of prison constitutively shapes the operations of workfare, as the two work hand in hand to sort the deserving from the undeserving poor. In this way, he argues, the non-incarcerated poor are treated "as *cultural similes of criminals*" (60). For this reason, we might see how our Shakespearean teaching documentaries, in the wake of PRWORA, are constitutively related to and dependent upon the genre of films depicting prisoners rehabilitated by Shakespeare. In fact, the punitive carceral state, functioning as a structuring absence or a margin conditioning a center, haunts many of our teaching documentaries, as their participants and their families regularly engage with prisons and courts. Much of *Romeo Is Bleeding* consists of interviews with police officers who track and report on the families and friends of those putting on the play. Police documents reporting the death and incarceration of those in and adjacent to the production regularly appear throughout the film, so much so that they feel like chapter breaks. The actor playing Romeo in *Ballet Changed My Life* often misses rehearsal for court dates and is almost forced to leave the production when he faces jail time. Despite the discourses of inclusion embraced by all of these films, in fact, many students are weeded out and asked to leave, forced to leave of necessity, or volunteer to leave the production, and in this way the films function, like PRWORA, to separate the ostensibly deserving from the undeserving poor. In his Teach for America lecture, depicted in *The Hobart Shakespeareans*, Esquith is candid about exclusion, telling the audience, "I want to let you know that some children *should* be left behind, *sorry*." He continues, arguing that once students are given an equal opportunity, "the children have to produce." Echoing the workfare logic of PRWORA, he contends that within his money system, "if you don't work, you don't get paid."

The "cultural simile of criminals" deeply structures no-excuses schools. In his book on the new paternalism, Whitman lays out an analogy comparing no-excuses schools with the largely discredited and hugely destructive "broken windows" theory of crime reduction, a theory that led to "stop-and-frisk" policies later found to be devastating to communities of color and unconstitutional in their execution. Whitman explains the new paternalism and no-excuses schools' mission:

> [Paternalistic schools] unapologetically insist that students adhere to middle-class virtues and explicitly rebuff the culture of the street . . . .In class, teachers constantly monitor whether students are tracking them with their eyes, whether students nod their heads to show that they are listening, and if any students have slouched in their seats. Teachers repeatedly admonish students to sit up, listen, nod, and track their speakers with their eyes [This series of actions is so regulated that it is simply referred to as "SLANT"]. Looking inattentive, or merely tapping a pen on a desk, can lead to students losing "scholar dollars" from virtual "paychecks" that can be used to earn special privileges at school (*Sweating* 21, 37–38).

With their emphasis on "character education" (an ostensibly secularized version of moral education), the new paternalist schools micromanage students' appearance, comportment, emotional labor, and affective relations. Young women are told: "hoop earrings can be no larger than a quarter ... In their personal hygiene class, girls learn to pluck the full eyebrow, to wipe away laganas ("eye boogers") every morning, to turn away when they blow their nose [*sic*], and to practice applying lip liner" (260–261). Students are trained to properly answer phones, firmly shake hands, and dine using proper etiquette. Whitman writes that the "new paternalistic schools are cultural evangelists: they build up the 'cultural capital' of low-income students by taking them to concerts, Shakespearean plays, college campus tours, and on trips to Washington, D.C. and national parks" (38). In *The Hobart Shakespeareans*, Esquith remarks that every year he takes his students on field trips to Washington, DC. The film and class website provide photographs of the students visiting the Folger Shakespeare Library. This annual trip (a pilgrimage of sorts) is supplemented by another trip to Colonial Williamsburg, Gettysburg, or Mount Rushmore. The film shows us a series of images chronicling these trips, and we follow Esquith's current students on their trips to UCLA and Washington, DC. Esquith tells us that people often ask why his students, "unpolished jewels," have such "poise and polish," and he explains that they get it "from the road." When the students board the bus to return home, Esquith snidely asks if they're excited to return home, to which the students respond in unison, "No!" He asks if they're excited to return to their "nice neighborhood," to which they reply, "No!" We see them "reject the culture" of their neighborhood in favor of a national "culture of excellence."

These neoliberal reforms are equally at home within Britain's New Labour government. Unsurprisingly, we also find the logic of no-excuses schools and the new paternalism in British Shakespeare documentaries. *Ballet Changed My Life: Ballet Hoo!* (2006), a reality series codirected by Michael Waldeman and Claire Lasko, the former of whom also directed *My Shakespeare* (2004), aired on Channel 4 in the United Kingdom. The series begins by announcing its premise: "From four local authorities in Birmingham and the Black Country, 200 young people embarked on an extraordinary journey. Alongside the tough love methods of the charity Youth at Risk, Birmingham Ballet put them through their paces. Those that stuck with it would have a chance to take part in a full performance of the ballet *Romeo and Juliet*." The ethos of Youth at Risk's program is delivered to viewers through the near-constant presence of the series' narrator, who tells us that "the Youth at Risk techniques are tough and confrontational. They make the young people face up to the consequences of their actions." The program's hope is that "[t]he discipline they'll need to learn in ballet should encourage greater self-discipline in their lives." The new paternalist policies, in the film, combine with the demands of emotional capitalism: "They have to keep rigorously to the rules: no hats, no food, no gum, no drinks, no swearing, and they have to be prepared to open up about their feelings."

The discourses of self-help continue throughout the film, in its narration and in its diegesis. The very idea of self-help seems paradoxical, at first: if the disciplinary force comes from a charity like Youth at Risk, or from bestselling literature, how is this truly "self" help? Part of the obsession with self-help culture under neoliberal conditions arises from our disavowal of heteronomy in the name of autonomy; help from others is rebranded as helping oneself. On the other hand, these disciplinary discourses can appropriately be called "self-help," in the sense that their "do-it-yourself" ethos does in fact center on the self as a locus of solutions to systemic problems. So, even if the 200 youth in *Ballet Changed My Life* are part of the same community, each is figured to be on his or her own path. Micki McGee has shown how, historically, a vast majority of self-help literature draws upon a set of shared metaphors: life as a path or journey, life as a spiritual calling, fashioning a life as a work of art, etc. From the very beginning of episode one, the narrator tells us that the youth are "setting out on a journey" on what will not be "an easy road" in their "long voyage to the stage." They will have to "face up to tough issues in their lives and talk about them openly" in order to get their "lives back on track" and continue on "this extraordinary mission." When Will Daniel-Braham, a white man and one of Youth at Risk's leading life coaches, wants to discipline a young black man named David for wearing jewelry and a hat, David asks why others can wear theirs. Will responds, "Don't worry about anyone else. It's all about you."

As opening night approaches, the ballet's director, Desmond Kelly, and the Youth at Risk life coaches become more paternalistic in the sense Whitman describes. The narrator tells us, "from now on, no excuses will be accepted for missing a rehearsal" or arriving late. Daniel-Braham introduces a "three-strikes rule" to the group, under which participants, after three infractions, lose their role; they do, however, have the opportunity to work with their coaches to appeal the decision. The logic and terminology of this "three-strikes rule" seems drawn from the growing popularity of "three-strikes statutes" or "perpetual offender" laws established in order to mandate life sentences to violent offenders. At rehearsal, Duane, a young black man who plays the role of the Prince, seems despondent. He has missed a number of rehearsals in order to appear at court for brandishing a knife at home. He is on probation and faces a five-year prison term. When Daniel-Braham tells him to "sit up" (or SLANT), he refuses and tells him he'll take a strike. The confrontation escalates, and after Duane is taken outside to discuss his case, we learn why he was so upset. It turns out that Duane had earlier that day received a letter telling him he had violated his probation and needed to return to court. Ultimately, we learn the letter was sent in error. However, it's not difficult to see how the disciplinary regime of *Ballet Changed My Life* is by no means an escape from the three-strikes and broken-windows ethos of the prisons and the courts. It is, rather, an extension of that ethos.

But no-excuses paternalism is not simply punitive or repressive; its powers – like all disciplinary power, as Foucault reminds us – are productive. Foucault writes, "We must cease once and for all to describe the effects of power in negative terms: it 'excludes,' it 'represses' ... In fact, power produces ... The individual and the knowledge that may be gained of him belong to this production" (*Discipline* 194). No-excuses and "broken-windows" policing focus on what Foucault describes as a "political anatomy of detail," a "micro-physics" of power that aims to produce obedient and emotionally enthusiastic subjects (139). Life coach Will Daniel-Braham features prominently in *Ballet Changed My Life*. His personal website lists his credentials in neurolinguistic programming or NLP, a pseudoscience with roots in the human potential movement of the 1960s. In her discussion of another NLP guru, Tony Robbins, Micki McGee describes NLP as an innovation that combines the "mind power" movement of the nineteenth century with new "scientific, cybernetic legitimacy": "In a blend of Pavlovian behavior modification and cybernetic language, neurolinguistic programming proposes that desired behaviors and feelings can be 'installed': that human emotion and action can be programmed as simply as software is installed in a computer" (60). Throughout the film, Daniel-Braham discusses the need for the youth in his charge to change the stories they tell about themselves (more on this in Section 4). Such behaviorist interventions seem to align with what critics of the daddy state have described as its "dehumanizing approach toward citizens that smacks of the behavioral science of B.F. Skinner" (Starobin 679). Ben-Ishai illustrates how new paternalism's self-help peda-gogy works to produce optimized laboring subjects: "insofar as new patern-alists aim to 'optimize' poor people's behavior – aligning intention to action – such programs use paternalism not in a restrictive manner but in a manner that reforms 'the self'" (155).

Though it may seem that responsibility is shifted exclusively to the individual, the self in need of help, in many of these films, family is equally important, especially fathers. The daddy state is more than just a metaphor. Melinda Cooper warns us that critiques of neoliberalism that focus exclusively on the individual ignore "the recurrent elision between the personal and the familial in neoliberal discourse," and thereby make "unintelligible its historical compatibility with various complexities of moral conservatism" (71). What's more, the framers of welfare "reform" share this "focus on the family" with every therapeutic discourse since Freud. In this respect, the figuration of Shakespeare as a *patrilineal inheritance*, which occurs frequently in a surprising number of these films, takes on added importance, as it sits at the intersection of the discourses of psychology and social welfare. Michael D. Bristol, in his book *Shakespeare's America, America's Shakespeare*, writes, "The idea that Shakespeare is a founder or creator of a specifically American experience of individuality and of collective life is articulated by Ralph Waldo Emerson, who described him famously as 'the father of the man in America'" (3).

In many of these documentaries, Shakespeare serves as a surrogate and metonym for fathers. In *The Hobart Shakespeareans*, Esquith exclaims, "I love Shakespeare because my father read it to me as my bedtime story when I was a little boy. It's what I was raised on." In *Why Shakespeare?* many of the interview subjects invoke these paternal memories. For example, poet David St. John reminisces, telling students, "My father would read [me] Shakespeare, his father read him Shakespeare." St. John calls Shakespeare a "gift . . . a parent gives you." Journalist Miles Beller tells us that, when he was in seventh grade, his father took him to see *Rosencrantz and Guildenstern Are Dead*, and he was "transformed." In the United Kingdom, where we might more readily expect to find Shakespeare framed as a patrilineal inheritance, we see a similar obsession with absent fathers whose role is fulfilled by Shakespeare. The narrator of *Ballet Changed My Life* tells us, "The nature of the relationship with their fathers is a recurring theme in these teenagers' lives." Eshe, who ultimately leaves the ballet, tells us that in her home, there "was no dad around." David, who plays Lord Capulet, confesses to the group that "when you don't see your dad," it has a big effect on you. In playing Juliet's father, we're told, he will, through Shakespeare, "discover the father figure within himself." In *Shakespeare High*, Chris Marquez tells us that, because his father died, he is "playing the role model as a father" to his three siblings. One is continually struck by how these Shakespeare documentaries index the paternal anxieties of what we might now reimagine as the White Christian Shakespearean Oedipal Complex.

Margaret Thatcher famously declared, "There is no such thing as society." According to this logic, there are only individuals and families. Neoliberalism unites left and right in a consensus that families ought to be the locus of social responsibility, but this consensus is threatened by what both groups see as the breakdown of the traditional nuclear family. Melinda Cooper writes that, in the United States, "[m]uch like their conservative Christian peers, the communitarian New Democrats are obsessed with the decline of marriage, rising rates of illegitimate childbearing, and the resultant epidemic of 'fatherless families,' but they deploy conventional social science language methods to buttress their conclusions and carefully avoid the overtly antifeminist, homophobic language" (110). Such discourses, more recently shorn of their racial dimensions, have a long history in US public policy. In 1965, Daniel Patrick Moynihan published *The Negro Family: The Case for National Action*, a report in which he notoriously pathologized the matriarchal structure of black family life in the United States, describing it as a "tangle of pathology" (US Department of Labor 29). Moynihan, who cites and perpetuates the pathologizing discourse of E. Franklin Frazier's 1939 *The Negro Family*, describes the indices of family pathology in terms that continue to concern and structure our documentarians in the twenty-first century. Moynihan lists "every index of family pathology – divorce, separation, and desertion, female family head, children in broken homes, and illegitimacy," and though our films also index the problem of incarceration, all of the "pathologies" that Shakespeare is framed to help participants "transcend" are clearly rooted in the family (19). For that reason, the new paternalism, functioning as a paternal supplement, hopes to step in as a surrogate father even if Whitman also advises schools to not "demand much from parents" (*Sweating* 259). Worth noting here is that a vast majority of the teachers depicted in our Shakespearean documentaries, especially those films that revolve around a single teacher, are men. In *Shakespeare High*, however, where many of the drama teachers are women, Sarah Rosenberg, a teacher at PUC Charter School, claims, "The school is really like a giant mother. It takes care of them [and] protects them." When asked why the no-excuses schools adopt a "paternal" rather than "maternal" model, Whitman responds:

> These schools, overwhelmingly, are composed of students from single-parent families. They're living with their mother, with their aunt, with their grandma. And, not only are the fathers not living at home, they're also not married ... And not only is that true of their family, they're often growing up in neighborhoods where there are virtually no married couples raising children. And, these children by and large don't need the school to act like a surrogate mother. They have surr- they have mothers. What they need is some kind of guidance and teaching the development of mastery that fathers could help provide. (Whitman "David Whitman")

This ambiguous and assumed link between fathers and "mastery" is even more striking when we consider Hortense Spillers's critique of Moynihan. Writing about Frazier and Moynihan, Spillers argues that "family" – "as we practice and understand it 'in the West,'" as "the *vertical* transfer of a bloodline, of a patronymic, of titles and entitlements, of real estate and the prerogatives of 'cold cash,' from *fathers* to *sons*" – historically excluded the sons and daughters of slaves, even when the father of those children was the white slave master, a situation in which Spillers claims "the denied genetic link becomes the chief strategy of an undenied ownership" (76). The racially uneven historical link between paternity, property, and inheritance also takes on new importance if we consider that the neoliberal consensus around welfare "reform" has long been tethered to a rebuke of inheritance taxes, so-called "death taxes," even while "empirical data on wealth distribution suggests that inheritance is almost as decisive at the beginning of the twenty-first century as it was in the nineteenth" (Cooper 123).

Welfare "reform" – from Moynihan's report to Clinton's PRWORA, from the marriage incentive programs of the Bush era, to the responsible fatherhood programs so heavily supported by the Obama administration – against the figure of the powerful matriarch and the nanny state, substitutes the figure of the father as one whose mental hygiene will wash away pathology, as one whose discipline will modify the behavior of those unwilling to delay gratification, whose paternity will, through the discourses of self-help, transform and bring into the fold of middle-class respectability those historically excluded. This focus on patrilineal inheritance brings us back to the curious ubiquity of the figure of Henry V in these films, particularly the obsession with his speech at Agincourt, which appears at the climax of a number of these films. *Shakespeare in Our Time*, distributed by the NEA as part of its multimedia kit, ends with a montage intercutting Branagh's version of Henry's speech with the version performed in *Renaissance Man*. To make sense of the obsession with this speech, we must return to Capitol Hill on October 28, 2003, and to Gioia's emotional confession.

On that day, Rafe Esquith was in attendance on Capitol Hill alongside Dana Gioia and Laura Bush. Joining Esquith was a group of Hobart Elementary students who performed monologues at the ceremony. Also taking the stage that night were eight members of Congress who donned Elizabethan costumes and performed a skit composed of excerpts from Shakespeare plays. Unlike the students, however, the congressional actors read from scripts. As Gioia narrates, *Why Shakespeare?* presents the viewer with footage of students in Rafe Esquith's classroom practicing fight choreography; this footage is intercut with still images of Hobart student Timothi Lee reciting the Saint Crispin's Day speech. In one of the photos,

Figure 4 Shakespeare in the US Capitol

Lee stands on Capitol Hill, sawing the air with his hand while an enormous SIAC logo towers directly behind him. The logo – the Droeshout portrait of Shakespeare emblazoned on an American flag – takes up one third of the frame, and the student's uplifted hand almost seems more Pentecostal than theatrical (see Figure 4). After Gioia is done narrating, the film presents yet another reenactment of the October event, as a different Hobart student recites the English monarch's call to war. At the end of the speech, as the actor's face begins to fade, we see an American flag in the background upon which – at the moment the soundtrack, trumpeting "Yeager's Triumph," the theme from both *The Right Stuff* and *Waiting for Superman*, builds to an affective crescendo – the SIAC logo leaps to the screen. Imagining the events of October 28, I cannot help but consider President Bush's similar call to arms, an event that occurred at a press conference earlier that day on Capitol Hill where Bush spoke on the situation in Iraq, where he was engaging in another mission to save and uplift a population raised in non-English-speaking homes (Office of the Press Secretary).

When we consider Gioia's narration in *Why Shakespeare?* we might note that what moves him to tears – the content of Henry's speech – is *itself* a pedagogical tale that involves the teaching and transmission of a patrilineal inheritance:

> This story shall the good man teach his son,
> And Crispin Crispian shall ne'er go by
> From this day to the ending of the world
> But we in it shall be remembered,
> We few, we happy few, we band of brothers.
> For he that sheds his blood with me
> Shall be my brother; be he ne'er so vile,
> This day shall gentle his condition. (*HV* 4.3.54–4.3.63)

Henry claims that "this story shall the good man teach his son," the telling of which will allow the patronyms of these patriarchs, through their sons, to be "freshly remembered" after others, those excluded and undeserving who "hold their manhoods cheap," are long forgotten (4.3.66). Shakespeare, in these films, works as a similar tale, one to be passed down from fathers to sons. Within the narrative of *Henry V*, English honor, embodied in the horizontally aligned fratriarchy of the "band of brothers," in order to survive, must be passed down vertically, that is, patrilineally through the generations. The preservation of honor depends upon the unimpeded repetition of a tale that, each time it is told, allows the honor of this fratriarchy/patriarchy to be "freshly remembered." This is the Shakespeare desired and presented by the NEA's films. "Shakespeare for a New Generation" is both the name of the NEA program and the subtitle of *My Shakespeare: Romeo and Juliet for a New Generation*. Participation in this fraternal order will transform its members, incorporating the "vile" and "gentl[ing their] condition." Like Henry, with a little self-help and paternal guidance, their "reformation, glit'ring o'er [their] fault, / Shall show more goodly and attract more eyes" (*1H4* 1.2.208). Most important, though, is the fact that what moves Gioia here is *not* simply Henry's speech, but the fact that a young boy, as he says, "raised in a non-English-speaking home," through Shakespeare, appears to have heeded Henry's call and been interpellated into a national patriarchal heritage. Perhaps this heritage is what Esquith's euphemistic "culture of excellence" truly stands in for.

Worth noting here, however, is that Dana Gioia himself did not learn Shakespeare from his father. Alternatively, he recalls his childhood memory of Shakespeare this way: "I remember my Mexican-American mother reciting passages of Shakespeare that she had to memorize in school, which awakened me in some ways to poetry." However, in eighth grade, his teacher, a nun, could not understand what he was saying, so she held him and a friend after class. Gioia remembers, "She made us memorize a dialogue from Shakespeare as training in diction, to teach us how to speak in a way people could understand." Through memorization, Gioia's incomprehensible mother tongue was tamed as he learned again "how to speak." Lee, whose father, we learn, did not read him Shakespeare, occupies a similar position within the historical trajectory of this patrilineal American inheritance. As an outsider, his presence "in the US Capitol" highlights the precariousness of the process of interpellation, threatening, as it does, an end to the seamless historical transmission of a particular set of values, values cloaked under the mantle of "excellence." Many of these films seem intent on neutralizing such threats. With the notable and partial exception of *Romeo Is Bleeding*, contemporary Shakespearean teaching documentaries efface cultural and historical difference in the name of a universal and timeless culture of excellence. In their important book, *Teaching Shakespeare with Purpose: A Student-Centered Approach*, Ayanna Thompson and Laura Turchi ask, "Who benefits from a race-free, gender-free, sexuality-free and ability-free approach [to Shakespeare instruction]? Who is at an advantage if students are discouraged from sharing observations about identity politics in the plays or in the classroom?" (13). Thompson and Turchi turn our attention to many of the pedagogical problems that also plague the films in question. They caution that Shakespeare instruction too often suffers from being "inadvertently avoidant, reductive and authoritarian" – avoidant in that it eschews the difficulty of the texts in favor of biography or abstract themes, reductive in that it aims to simplify or translate Shakespeare's complexity, and authoritarian in that teachers too readily assume the burden of explaining (away) such complexity (45–46). Thompson and Turchi identify two important problems related to the value of teaching Shakespeare: "claims for the texts' universality and assumptions about their relevance" (48). They argue, "If universality erases history, relevance erases the text. We value Shakespeare's texts precisely because they illuminate the difficult correspondences between the specific language of the characters and the specific lives of students" (49). Their book goes a long way in mapping out an alternative approach to Shakespeare in the classroom, an approach that, if documented, would produce a stunningly original film. One does get the sense, watching contemporary Shakespearean teaching films, that the student performers, whose diversity is nevertheless always foregrounded, must have struggled with the plays in ways informed by the specificity of their lived experience, that they must have encountered Shakespeare's difficulty and labored productively and imaginatively to connect his alien world to theirs. However, these films do not yet seem to know how to show us what such a student-centered approach, one that truly values encounters with difference, might look like. Such moments are only rarely or partially depicted, and when they are, particularity quickly melts into abstraction as diversity is subsumed by "excellence." Within these films, cultural and historical differences recede into the background as the films foreground students' transcendental relationship with Shakespeare, a relationship framed within the limited contours of the White Christian Shakespeare Complex's conversion narrative.

4 Character Education and Spiritual-Therapeutic Conversion Narratives

The obsession with Prince Hal evidenced in our films, and in the literatures promoting Shakespearean insights in business, are curiously mirrored in discourses around George W. Bush's presidency. Especially after Bush's bullhorn speech at Ground Zero after 9/11, the media and especially the right became frenzied with comparisons between Bush and Henry V, both of whom redeemed their wayward youths by reviving their fathers' legacies

(Newstok [Newstrom]). Most of these discussions were framed around Bush reviving his father's designs on Iraq, but Bush's NCLB initiative also brought his father's educational plans into fruition (Erickson 92). Prince Hal, in these Shakespearean documentaries, seems to function as the prototypical youth reformed and redeemed in his father's image. At the beginning of *King Henry V*, the Archbishop of Canterbury describes his miraculous transformation. Audiences, however, know that Canterbury's perspective on Hal's performance of redemption, much like the point of view taken by our films, is distorted, seen as it is through the lens of the White Christian Savior Complex:

> The courses of his youth promised it not.
> The breath no sooner left his father's body
> But that his wildness, mortified in him,
> Seemed to die too; yea, at that very
>   moment,
> Consideration like an angel came
> And whipped th'offending Adam out of
>   him,
> Leaving his body as a paradise
> T'envelop and contain celestial spirits.
> Never was such a sudden scholar made,
> Never came reformation in a flood
> With such heady currence scouring faults,
> Nor never Hydra-headed willfulness
> So soon did lose his seat, and all at once,
> As in this king. (1.1.24–1.1.37)

The catalyst for this ostensible transformation, the death of the father, Henry IV, occurs in the same moment as ("at that very moment" "and all at once") transcendental intervention. Hal's antediluvian faults are washed away by "reformation in a flood," which scours his faults, the "offending Adam," and restores him to a prelapsarian moment of promise, making "his body as a paradise." This is perhaps "restoration" more than "reformation." The religious dimensions of this reformation, staged within the larger Protestant Reformation, are clear. However, what is less clear within this theological discourse, and within our films, are the class dimensions that align Henry with Bush more than with today's marginalized youth: both Henry and Bush were born into privilege and yet both are cast as triumphant underdogs, examples perhaps of how audiences tend to identify with the rich – a cruel optimism, to be sure. Bishop Ely says that Hal is like "the strawberry [that] grows underneath the nettle ... Neighbored by fruit of baser quality" (*H5* 1.1.60, 62), a sentiment that parallels – albeit perhaps more parasitically – the claim of Donté Clark, of *Romeo Is Bleeding*, that he is like "the rose that grew from concrete" – an image borrowed from rapper Tupac Shakur's song "The Rose That Grew from Concrete." Both images acknowledge the pressures of hierarchy but celebrate individual triumph over hierarchy, the crucial difference being that Hal, unlike Tupac or Clark, inherits his privilege and so his rise is less a miracle than such figures suggest.

Within a British context, where class consciousness operates differently, the power of patrilineally inherited privilege is perhaps more salient, as in Laura Wade's 2010 play *Posh*, which was adapted for the screen as *The Riot Club* (2014). Wade appropriates, revises, and demystifies Prince Hal's tale by making the class dimensions more visible than ever. Members of the Riot Club (a fictionalization of Oxford's Bullingdon Club, former members of which – David Cameron, Boris Johnson, George Osborn, and Nick Hurd – now populate Britain's highest levels of government) take over the Bull's Head Inn (standing in for the Boar's Head Inn) in a night of violent revels and debauchery. As the Riot Club prepares for the main course, Hugo takes "a turn for the *iambic*," and gives a speech patterned on Hal's speech at Harfleur:

> Once more into the drink, dear friends, once more,
> And give a roar for all our English drunk ...
>   On, on, you noblest riot,
> Whose blood is fet from vodka 80 proof! ...
> Dishonour not dead members; now attest
> That Knights like our Lord Riot did beget you.

Be envy now to clubs of weaker blood,
And teach them how to drink. The game's afoot!
Pour out your spirits, and with glasses charged,
Cry "God for Harry, Dimitri and Alistair, James, Toby,
Edward, Milo, Hugo, Guy and George!" (Wade 66–67)

Throughout Act I the club members puff themselves up and vent their anger at the bourgeoisie and the poor until the scene ends with Alistair yelling, "I mean I am sick, I am sick to fucking death of *poor people*" (101). In Act II, this rage finds its target. In a Lord-of-the-Flies frenzy, the students beat the inn's proprietor nearly to death in a scene that echoes and highlights the classed violence Hal directs at Falstaff – and poor Francis the barkeep! – in Shakespeare's play.

Unlike most appropriations of Hal, the play has clearly decided to read Hal's reformation cynically by highlighting inherited privilege or what is today called "affluenza." Prince Hal's reformation, like many of the scenes I've taken up here, can be and has been read both cynically and sympathetically. Hazlitt, in 1817, calls Hal an "amiable monster"; Gerald Gould, in 1919, writes that "*Henry V* is a satire on monarchical government, on imperialism, on the baser kinds of 'patriotism,' and on war"; and Alan Sinfield and Jonathan Dollimore argue that "even in this play, which is often assumed to be the one where Shakespeare is closest to state propaganda, the construction of ideology is complex – even as it consolidates, it betrays inherent instability" (qtd. in Craik 71, 72, 79). However, religious discourses – which value conversion, transformation, noble character, and divine providence – along with therapeutic discourses – which value self-actualization, self-optimization, and triumph over trauma – make such cynical readings, readings that might question such narratives by acknowledging structural inequality along raced and classed lines, harder to come by. My goal in this section is to show how these films are shaped by such religious and therapeutic discourses and how, because of this, they do not allow us to acknowledge or imagine broader and more political forms of collective harm or care.

In his book on supervisory approaches to the poor, Lawrence Mead is explicit about how the new paternalism aims to efface race. Mead writes that "paternalism is really a postracial social policy ... The most important causes of black poverty appear to lie in the past" (22). Following Mead, David Whitman contends that the new paternalism will soon be "denuded of many of its racial overtones" as it takes on a more "liberal hue." This will happen because the leaders of these schools and their teachers, most of whom, we learn, are "white, liberal, and young," have "little personal experience with poverty" or with "the identity politics of the 1970s and 1980s. When Dave Levin [who studied with Rafe Esquith before founding KIPP] was a sophomore in college, the Moynihan report was already 25 years old." With these political considerations now a thing of the past, today's "new paternalists [can become] like modern-day missionaries, ready to have a few doors slammed in their faces as they try to spread the gospel of transformational urban school reform" (*Sweating* 66–67). Here, as in our films and in Shakespeare's tale of Hal's reformation, religious discourses obscure the respective raced and classed political terrains upon which transformation is imagined to occur.

What I earlier called the White Christian Shakespeare Complex is rooted in the big emotional payoff white saviors – and viewers – feel when engaging in underdog politics denuded of larger political dimensions, but it's important to further explore the Christian roots of this problematic, what makes it a *Christian* complex. Primary here is a consideration of the role of the Protestant work ethic. Whitman explicitly states that no-excuses schools aim to instill "middle-class values and the Protestant work ethic" (*Sweating* 260). Micki McGee's study of self-help literature likewise argues that imperatives to optimize the self and discover the right career "path" build on the Protestant notion of the "calling" as explored by Max Weber (25). The narrator of *Ballet Changed My Life* describes the "journey" of the film's youth as an "extraordinary mission." When *Romeo Is Bleeding*'s Donté Clark discovers spoken word poetry, he realizes he can move his audience to tears; he tells us "people started crying." Clark's brother tells us that a life of gangs and drugs was "in his bloodline" and that "he was heading that way." Clark confesses to the audience that the discovery of poetry inspired an epiphany. He says, "I changed – I changed my profession." Later, he tells us, "I felt resurrected." Evangelical conversion narratives, an emergent and increasingly popular genre at the turn of the seventeenth century, follow this same narrative pattern. Like Clark's sudden change of heart and course, conversion narratives are similarly structured around a sudden "conversion of the heart," one that results in a "turning from and a turning to" (Hindmarsh 32, 14). Over time, the evangelical conversion narrative acquires, through the testimonies of ex-slaves, an additional, racial dimension as it builds upon the "biblical theme of emancipation and freedom from bondage" (332). In our documentaries, however, it's Shakespeare who converts and emancipates.

McGee argues that religious traditions form a continuous, if unevenly avowed, backdrop animating self-help discourses, noting that "the Bible is perhaps the first and most significant of self-help books" (5). She cites self-help guru Tony Robbins, who claims that self-help infomercials and programing arose when Christian televangelists' ratings fell in the mid-1990s; he proclaims: "We are the new televangelists" (59). Byung-chul Han elaborates on the homologies between Protestant self-scrutiny and self-help discourses' imperative to optimize the self:

> The neoliberal ideology of self-optimization displays religious – indeed, fanatical – traits ... Endlessly working at self-improvement resembles the self-examination and self-monitoring of Protestantism ... Now, instead of searching out sins, one hunts down negative thoughts. The ego grapples with itself as an enemy. Today, even fundamentalist preachers act like managers and motivational trainers, proclaiming the new Gospel of limitless achievement and optimization. (30)

In these films, the arts in general and Shakespeare in particular are recruited in the service of self-optimization – or, perhaps, what markets itself as "self-optimization" but is really only the optimization of the successful worker producing under capital for others. This optimization-for-capital, however, is framed as self-help or self-actualization. Dana Gioia, in *Why Shakespeare?*, claims that art teaches you to "learn to be authentically yourself ... who [you] really are." Summoning the figure of self-optimization as a path, he continues: "there are many paths to success, many paths to self-realization ... multiple ways to excellence." These abstractions – paths, success, self-realization, excellence – stand in for and obscure the concrete circumstances of these films' underdogs. McGee correctly points out that "in the absence of a social safety net and in the face of profound economic injustice, any discussion of self-actualization is rendered absurd. Even the psychologist, Abraham Maslow, who popularized this term, would consider the pursuit of self-actualization without some measure of economic security to be a tenuous, if not impossible, undertaking" (183).

Nevertheless, these films, and the no-excuses new paternalist logic to which most subscribe, figure Shakespeare and performance as a way out of impossible circumstances, and it is Shakespeare's difficulty, and the discipline required to master his drama, that promises to gentle the condition of our underdogs. Ayanna Thompson sums up the imagining of Shakespeare as a vehicle for reform best when she tells us that the "logic behind this rhetoric is, of course, familiar by now: Shakespeare = difficult = good for you" (141). In *Professing Literature: An Institutional History*, Gerald Graff notes that such paradigms, like so much else being revised and refashioned in our films, are an inheritance of the nineteenth century: "The most frequently stated justification for the way the classics were taught was the theory of 'mental discipline,' which was rooted in the mechanistic faculty psychology of the nineteenth century. The theory presumed that, like the body, the mind and character are strengthened by strenuous, repetitive exercise on disagreeably difficult tasks" (30). The narrator for *Ballet Changed My Life* similarly explains that "the hope" of their endeavor "is that remorseless discipline and repetition will help" transform the lives of participants. Desmond Kelly, the ballet's director, makes the astonishing claim that "These young people are not used to being disciplined; they're not used to being shouted at, and told 'Go over there and do that now.'" In fact, these young people are probably more used to such discipline than Kelly. When one of the youths, David, gets frustrated by such "remorseless discipline," he walks out of rehearsal. After meeting with his coach, the narrator informs us that "David has begun to realize that being told what to do isn't always a bad thing."

The narrator of *Ballet Changed My Life* tells us that the world of ballet will provide these youths with "a world different from their everyday lives, one of commitment, perseverance, and precision. At stake here is whether art can change lives." While art certainly does have the potential to change lives, in so many of these films art's utility lies in its ability to teach *perseverance in the face of adversity*, as though this is not something the youths might teach their benefactors. The education "reform" movement following NCLB welcomed the popularity of psychologist and MacArthur Genius Angela Duckworth's *New York Times* bestseller *Grit: The Power of Passion and Perseverance*. Written like a self-help book, complete with diagrams and a "grit scale" readers can use to measure their own grit, the book surveys successful people and provides anecdotal stories garnered during the author's quest to show how passion and perseverance are better indicators of lifetime achievement than IQ (much as Goleman's *Emotional Intelligence* sought to displace IQ with EQ). Duckworth draws on the insights of cognitive behavioral therapy, the history of philosophy, and advice from CEOs like Wendy Kopp of Teach for America and Bill McNabb of Vanguard, popularizer of the classroom money scheme discussed earlier. She also draws on the insights of Dave Levin and Michael Feinberg, the "two gritty young Teach for American teachers" who founded KIPP after working with Rafe Esquith (101). In the book she tells of being approached by an eager young entrepreneur at the Wharton School of Business. Echoing Rafe Esquith's class motto and his vacuous appeals, she tells the student, "there are no shortcuts to excellence." The young student, eager to impress Duckworth, tells her how hard he has been working on his current venture. She replies, "[I]f you're working on that project with the same energy in a year or two, email me." When the student answers that he might move on to a new project in a few years, she responds that she's "not sure [his] story illustrates grit." He asks, "You mean, stay in one company?" and she advises that "skipping around from one kind of pursuit to another – from one skill set to an entirely different one – that's not what gritty people do" (36).

Duckworth, like Whitman in his treatise on new paternalism in schools, stresses how underdogs can achieve when they combine passionate emotional labor with perseverance and self-control, which, together, allow one to delay immediate gratification. Whitman seems to share Duckworth's dangerous assumptions about those who do not succeed when he brazenly refers to the "inability to 'defer gratification' emblematic of 'underclass' culture" (51). However, what Duckworth and Whitman do not seem to understand is that such values no longer answer the demands of late capitalism's gig economy, with its precarious labor force constantly adapting and reinventing itself according to the fickle needs of the market. Here, the student's question – "You mean, stay in one company?" – speaks to the outmoded economic landscape to which grit stubbornly continues to respond. Richard Sennett, writing in 2006, ten years before Duckworth, makes this corrective in his *The Culture of the New Capitalism*: "Delayed gratification makes possible self-discipline; you steel yourself to work, unhappily or not, because you are focused on that future reward. This highly personalized version of the prestige of work requires a certain kind of institution to be credible ... The new paradigm makes nonsense of delayed gratification as a principle of self-discipline; those institutional conditions are missing" (77–78). Duckworth and Whitman renew and rehearse nineteenth-century discourses of perseverance and grit in order to shift onto the poor the responsibility for their own marginalization. Under contemporary conditions, such values are outdated and inefficient, if not dangerous.[7] Surely art can do more.

As neoliberal reforms slowly peel away the care provisions of the welfare state, neoliberal states on both sides of the Atlantic have reinvented and reinvigorated the role that privatized and religious forms of charity once played in the nineteenth century. This return, however, combines religious charity with twentieth-century innovations. As we saw earlier, Rafe Esquith's motto – "Be nice. Work hard." – combines the Taylorist logic of workfare efficiency with affective demands of twentieth-century emotional capitalism. Eva Illouz argues that Elton Mayo's workplace studies supplemented the Taylorist logic of the workplace with an attention to workers' emotional needs: "In place of the Victorian language of 'character,' Mayo used the amoral and scientific language of psychology to conceive of human relations as technical problems to be alleviated by proper knowledge and understanding" (69). However, I would argue that Christian notions of moral character do not recede as much as they are

---

[7] Many studies within the field of psychology conducted since the grit fad have shown that grit alone does not, in fact, consistently account for student success in the way Duckworth suggests. For one such study, see Credé et al.

combined with the "scientific language of psychology." This combination takes the form of an ostensibly secular and yet deeply religious "character education movement." The character education movement in the United States, according to Megan Boler, "is usually dated 1920–40, but is rooted in the mid-Victorian values that establish higher education institutions prior to the turn of the century" (48). Boler cites the eugenicist mental hygiene movement (whose proponents have been described as "evangelical") and the character education movement as the "[t]wo movements in education [that] sought to control emotions in the early part of the century" (48).

The idea of "character education" is as old as education itself. Throughout its history, it has had many names: from "religious education" to "moral education," to "civic education" and "service learning." While the term "character education" arose as a somewhat euphemistic secularization of Christian instruction, it is rooted in Protestant schools' attempts, in the mid-nineteenth century, to incorporate and assimilate immigrant Catholics (Howard, Berkowitz, and Schaeffer 191). In the America of the 1830s, with the expansion of free public schools, character education attempted to reinforce the "values of the home" in common schools; most important was that "the children of others – particularly immigrants – learn and practice them as well" (190). Character education experienced a resurgence in the late twentieth century at a moment concomitant with the rise of the Shakespeare documentary. Although Reagan was first to invest in character education, Clinton tripled federal funding for such programs (Watz 34). Importantly, his Charitable Choice provision of 1996 began a wave of legislation blurring the line between church and state, giving religious institutions and religious discourses many of the powers they held in the nineteenth century, what Melinda Cooper calls a "*reinstitutionalization of religion,* a process whereby religious charities resumed their once central role in the management of poverty but this time more fully integrated into the contractual networks and budgetary calculations of the state" (295). Cooper is worth quoting at length:

> The Charitable Choice provision of 1996, followed by the faith-based initiatives of George W. Bush and Obama [e.g., the White House Office for Faith-Based and Community or

Neighborhood Initiatives], have facilitated a dramatic expansion of the number of religious organizations engaged in the provision of social services ranging from homeless shelters, prison and post-prison reentry programs, drug rehabilitation services, welfare-to-work training, disaster relief, and sex (abstinence) education, along with marriage and responsible fatherhood programs. In the wake of welfare reform, the moral and economic obligations of work and family have been refashioned in the religious idiom of faith, conversion, and redemption. (271)

As Cooper illustrates, not only have religious and civic institutions joined in public-private partnerships, but the way we speak of and imagine social welfare has also been "refashioned" by religious discourses. Cooper cites conservative Leslie Lenkowsky who, dismayed by the "moral tone" of the Bush administration's implementation of Charitable Choice, describes it as "a throwback to an era when the nation's charities were concerned not just about the material circumstances of those they helped but about their character and behavior as well" (310).

This moral tone is perhaps nowhere more evident than in the rebirth of character education under the Bush administration. Bush's No Child Left Behind Act reauthorized and strengthened the Partnerships in Character Education Program, an initiative of the Department of Education. Between 1995 and 2005, the Department of Education spent $27 million on character education programs (Smagorinsky and Taxel 22). By 2005, forty-eight states had introduced character education programs. Some states even go as far as mandating the "virtues" or "character traits" that are to be taught. For example, Georgia's education code focuses on the following traits: "courage, patriotism, citizenship . . . punctuality, cleanliness, cheerfulness, school pride, respect for the environment, respect for the creator, patience, creativity, sportsmanship, loyalty, perseverance, and virtue" (Glanzer and Milson 531). Of character education, Bush said the following: "Every child must be taught these principles. Every citizen must uphold them, and every immigrant, by embracing these ideals, makes our country more, not less, American . . . a nation of character" (qtd. in Butts 7).

In *The Hobart Shakespeareans*, Esquith tells us that his students "defy the culture both of their neighborhood and their country. They immerse themselves in a culture where people are good to each other, where hard work matters and character matters even more." Esquith's work-hard-be-nice motto has been appropriated by KIPP charter schools as the slogan for their character education program, which was designed in "collaboration with Dr. Angela Duckworth" and others ("Focus on Character"). Duckworth, importantly, is now the CEO of a company called Character Lab, whose website offers modules on social intelligence, grit, gratitude, and self-control, the latter teaching "strength of will" ("Self-Control"). This focus on strength of will finds a curious echo in the t-shirts worn by Esquith's students, which link grit and self-control to Shakespeare through their "Will Power!" slogan. KIPP advertises that a "focus on character has been the cornerstone of KIPP since we began and is still the essence of what we believe" ("Focus on Character").

During their revival, character education programs in the United States and the United Kingdom sought justification by citing crises of moral decline in youth. United States Senate Resolution 176 of 1998 states, "concerns about the character training of children have taken on a new sense of urgency as violence by and against youth threatens the physical and psychological well-being of the nation" (qtd. in Smagorinsky and Taxel 139). This, despite the fact that studies show a steady *decrease* in violence in schools leading up to the legislation (90–91). Character education tends to resurface during times of moral crisis, times in which the strength of national identity seems to be on the wane; that is to say, it resurfaces constantly. The rebirth of UK character education comes after its US renaissance, and it too cites moral decline. The University of Birmingham's Jubilee Centre for Character and Virtue, one of the "largest research institutions in character, virtue and virtue education ever under-taken," reports in 2015 that the "call for character building in UK schools increased in 2011 as riots occurred in several areas across the country. Prime Minister David Cameron (2011) claimed that the riots were caused by people 'showing indifference to right and wrong' and having 'a twisted moral code'" (Arthur et al. 8). Cameron, who apparently wants to keep rioting the privilege of his Bullingdon or "Riot" Club, invoked character education as a solution to what he called a "slow-motion moral collapse" (8). These riots, in fact, came in response to what the public perceived as a racist police shooting, a fact that complicates Cameron's moral absoluteness.

Cameron's comments are telling, as they reveal exactly who gets to riot and who must behave. Henry Giroux further exposes character education's uneven deployment: "Character education is not aimed at schools for the rich and privileged, who would hardly tolerate the strictures of such obedience training and modes of authoritarianism" (93). Traditional forms of character education concentrate on making students passive, obedient, patriotic, and respectful of authority. Giroux argues that a traditional character education approach "focuses on controlling individual behavior but totally neglects the relationship between individual behavior and the responsibilities of social life" (94). The traditional approach to character education is best represented by US conservative Thomas Lickona, who authors the preface of the University of Birmingham's study. Lickona, like Rafe Esquith, argues that "objectively good human qualities [and] basic human values transcend religious and cultural differences and express our common humanity ... our common moral ground, what unites us rather than what divides us" (23). Predictably, many objected to this desire to efface difference. B. E. McClellan writes that "this scheme showed little tolerance for cultural diversity, and there can be no doubt that reformers expected it to play an important role in eliminating the differences that set immigrants off from the mainstream American life" (qtd. in Howard et al. 191).

As character education evolved in the late twentieth century, it began to incorporate the therapeutic discourses of psychology. The so-called "values clarification school" grounded Lickona's transcendent values by emphasizing individual decision-making when faced with complex problems in difficult contexts. These new reformers were led by Jean Piaget's student Lawrence Kohlberg, and conservatives predictably responded to these new reforms with accusations of moral relativism. In a 1999 campaign speech, Bush bemoaned the fact that in schools, "Values were 'clarified,' not taught. Students were given moral puzzles, not moral guidance" (qtd. in Smagorinsky and Taxel 129). Bush, like Cameron, favors moral absoluteness.

Not all character education programs are politically conservative, and character education programs have been implemented differently and unevenly across space. For example, feminist critics of Kohlberg's positivist emphasis on the (usually white male) individual – critics like Carol Gilligan and Nel Noddings – have emphasized the value of "the affective," arguing that "moral emotions and sentiments" stimulate moral action as "care" (Howard et al. 195). In their study of character education's implementation in the United States, Smagorinsky and Taxel have shown that although character education programs might be politically diverse in approach, there is some consistency in how they are distributed geographically, with more traditional approaches being applied in the Deep South. There, the authors discover the traits of a very traditional character education: an emphasis on youth depravity, nostalgia for the past, anxiety about the composition of working-class and nonwhite families, moral absoluteness, obedience to authority, "the discourse of the virtuous individual" (190–200, 200). Programs in the Upper Midwest, however, emphasized citizenship, community, diversity, relationships, and student agency (279–287). Common in both regions, however, was the stress placed on the Protestant work ethic, and with this, unsurprisingly, the therapeutic discourses of self-help culture provided a framework for increased student productivity. We learn that one state licensed and implemented Stephen Covey's *7 Habits of Highly Effective People*, a "perfect fit" with the chosen model of character education (193).

When character education meets Shakespeare, the importance of character is doubled, as the characters within the play – most often stripped of their complexity – serve as representations of virtue and morality. At a 2002 White House Conference on Character and Community, Bush told his auditors, "it's an interesting idea – where virtues are taught by studying the great historical figures and characters in literature; and where consideration is encouraged and good manners are expected" ("Remarks at the White House Conference on Character and Community" 1021). The idea that contact with Shakespeare's drama imparts virtue is not new. The use of Shakespearean drama – full-length plays – to teach morality emerges most strongly at the end of the nineteenth century (Frey 521). In his study of Shakespeare instruction in America during the late nineteenth and early twentieth centuries, Charles Frey, citing Stephen J. Brown's "The Uses of Shakespeare in America: A Study in Class Domination," stakes out a perennial tension between, on the one hand, seeing Shakespeare "primarily as an instrument of class oppression, a tool for 'the imposition of white Anglo-Saxon Protestant civility from above'" and, on the other, Shakespeare's use as a tool for upward mobility (544). As the emphasis on complexity and close reading, dominant from Kittredge to the New Critics, came to a close, Frey tells us, another school, one dominated by Alfred Harbage, came to emphasize Shakespeare's simplicity, accessibility, and moral goodness, a shift that promoted the use of Shakespeare in secondary education. Frey writes, "With the arrival of Harbage the hounds of morality, so mercilessly held at bay by Kittredge, had returned with a vengeance," a move that marked a shift from "aesthetic-to-ethical interpretation" (550).

For the most part these documentaries frame Shakespeare as simple, accessible, and morally good. In *Why Shakespeare?* William Shatner tells us, "If you listen, and that's the key, you've got to listen . . . you'll get the meaning, and the meaning has universality." Carol Muske-Dukes asserts, "When I want guidance, I go to Shakespeare . . . I go to Shakespeare when I want to learn something about my life." Shakespeare is simply there, ready and available to all who seek him out. Shakespeare is, in fact, required reading in most secondary schools, a fact somehow disavowed by many of these films when they frame Shakespeare as something with which students have most likely never had contact. As Ayanna Thompson has argued regarding Shakespeare reform programs, the assumption that "the exposure is all" is common, as if these students were not already (perhaps repeatedly) exposed (134). Even when they do engage Shakespeare in these films, his plays are almost always presented as abstract analogies to contemporary concerns, a strategy by which the plays and the contemporary moment are stripped of their particularity. In *Romeo Is Bleeding*, the feud between aristocratic households is figured as being directly analogous to the gang warfare of Richmond's impoverished residents – violence is violence, in any context.

The idea of Shakespeare as an inherently moral and explicitly Christian resource for the teaching of virtue is also one we inherit from the nineteenth century, when "[m]any seriously advocated treating Shakespeare's works as a secular, national Bible" (Laporte 610). Charles Laporte provides a long list of publications in the nineteenth century drawing comparisons between Shakespeare and the Bible; he describes how "a small critical subgenre arises in mid-century to imply that Shakespeare more or less answers for the Bible and vice versa" (611). These texts, Laporte tells us, "reprint lines of Shakespeare in conjunction with (and sometimes directly alongside) parallel quotations from the Bible as though to imply their equivalence, often organizing them by thematic rubrics such as 'The Compensations of Adversity,' 'The Dangers of Idleness,' and 'The Value of a Good Name'" (611). The popularity and supposed value of these lessons – particularly as proffered by Christian elders to impoverished youth – has clearly not diminished in the twenty-first century.

In Lloyd Kramer's *Midsummer in Newtown* (2016), we hear from "three families who find hope in the transformative power of the arts." After the horrific massacre at Sandy Hook Elementary School, residents and students of Newtown are understandably grieving and dealing with trauma and loss. Kramer, who also directed a Mitch Albom documentary with Oprah Winfrey, follows Michael Unger, NewArts' artistic director, as he works with Sandy Hook students to put on a rock-and-roll production of *Midsummer Night's Dream*. Unger tells us, "I don't know how to restore faith in the world," but as the production moves on, the young people are transformed. Sammy Vertucci's mother reveals early on, "She's been not the same person since the whole event took place." At the end of the film, she says, "[Sammy] is able to look outside herself now. She leans in. She's more inviting to the world ... I almost have my prior-to-the-event Sammy back." Nine-year-old Tain lost a friend in the shooting. Despite his age, he will be playing Snug. Tain states that God is the most important thing in his life, and his parents also testify to his "strong sense of faith." His father tells us that "Tain's belief in God [has] helped him navigate these waters." The power of prayer is present throughout the film, but the power of Shakespeare seems to work similarly.

Although our Shakespeare documentaries only occasionally invoke religion directly, the confessional forms of student testimony – young people recounting their past difficulties in explicit detail, a recounting followed by the conversion narratives they offer after their transformative encounters with Shakespearean drama – feel directly related to self-help culture and its biblical antecedents. Whereas Philip Rieff famously declared that the twentieth century witnessed a "Triumph of the Therapeutic" over religious discourses, Micki McGee describes this as "a victory of assimilation or appropriation." She argues, "Psychotherapeutic notions of health and well-being were conflated with spiritual values of saintliness or goodness, while the Protestant religious imperative to pursue a calling was wedded to notions of mental health and psychological well-being" (42). Eva Illouz similarly argues that therapeutic discourses are modeled on what she calls "the basic cultural template of the Judeo-Christian narrative": "That template [is] both regressive and progressive: regressive because it is about past events that are, so to speak, still present and at work in people's lives, and progressive because the goal of the narrative is to establish prospective redemption, here, emotional health" (184). Our films repeatedly exhibit the regressive and progressive temporal logic of Christian confessional narratives, and they also seem to figure emotional health as a form of secular, if not spiritual, redemption.

The youth in these films recount, in great detail, the adverse circumstances of their youth. In *Shakespeare High*, in addition to three reformed gang members, we meet Galvin and Melvin Emisibe, twins who have lived in three foster homes since their father killed their mother. Galvin, valedictorian of his class, looks forward to enjoying a full scholarship at UC Davis. Most of our films, in fact, end prospectively by providing the viewer with a "Where are they now?" closing sequence. As with the Emisibes, in *Ballet Changed My Life*, a young woman named Shireenah admits to the group, "When I was two, my dad murdered my mom." The narrator asks: "Can ballet training make any difference for a fourteen-year-old whose dad killed her mum?" Shireenah's confession is replayed repeatedly throughout the series, as are the tearful confessions of others. The narrator tells us that these "are no ordinary teenagers. Some of them have endured abuse, violence, rape, neglect, and extreme poverty." Another young woman, Zara, tells the group, "I've been locked up, I've been in prison cells, I've robbed from shops." A young man named Anton tells the camera: "At the beginning, I was near my bottom, basically. Now, I'm actually seeing a future for myself. So, it's gone from, like, me being angry to learning something from it, and I think from that, it's made me stronger and more confident and more emotional, so I can relate to more people." Another youth, Duane, shares that early in life he was "naughty and bad." The narrator tells us that he committed a robbery with a knife, which led to a long and troubled relationship with jail and the courts. But Duane has been transformed. Whereas before, he was "a lawbreaker," now that he plays Prince Escalus, he says, "I'm the boss. I'm law and order."

Illouz describes how, by the 1990s, such therapeutically informed "confessional autobiographies became a well-established genre" (*Saving* 182). What's more, she claims that "the therapeutic narrative structures the mode of speech and confession in a genre which has emerged in the last 15 years and has transformed the entire medium of TV" (*Cold Intimacies* 50). This new genre "makes the public exposure of psychic suffering central to the account of oneself" (*Saving* 181). The public exposure of psychic suffering takes the form of what Lauren Berlant has called "testimonial rhetorics of true pain" ("Subject" 57). In no way do I here mean to question the veracity or value of such testimony or the very real violence spanning from Richmond to Newtown to Birmingham. As Berlant notes, questioning how such testimony functions can often seem tantamount to inflicting further violence (58). However, with Berlant, I want to problematize how, within our films, "[q]uestions of social inequity and social value" are "adjudicated in the register not of power but of sincere surplus feeling" (58). In these "testimonial rhetorics of true pain," we witness the personal, individual effects of systemic violence. While I have been arguing throughout that all of these films disavow or simply eschew issues of class and race, on the other hand, while they may not name these issues directly, these films appear obsessed with and anxious about race and class. Perhaps we might borrow insights from Foucault's critique of the repressive hypothesis in the first volume of his *History of Sexuality*.

Where we have imagined a censorship or repression of discourses of race and class, we might instead observe how our films obsessively discourse on inequality; however, they do so by other means. About class and racial inequality in our films, we might say with Foucault: "Not any less was said about it; on the contrary. But things were said in a different way; it was different people who said them, from different points of view, and in order to obtain different results" (*History* 27). By replacing, or better yet augmenting twentieth-century discourses on inequality, religious, pedagogical, therapeutic, documentarian and even theatrical discourses have merged to shape *how* we talk about race and class. Foucault writes of the "wide dispersion of devices that were invented for speaking about [sex], for having it be spoken about, for inducing it to speak of itself, for listening, recording, transcribing, and redistributing what is said about it" (34). We might say the same about race and class as taken up by our documentaries. Far from the early or midcentury discourses, which were rooted in "labor and capital," "oppression," "solidarity," "consciousness-raising," or "liberation," we now witness the rise of a new set of interlocking discourses with their own shared contours: the euphemistic passive voice – "at-risk" or "troubled" youth – the hyperbolic – "broken homes" and "transformations" – the metonymic and metaphorical – "latchkey kids," "nanny states," and "underdogs" – and the individualized – "will power," "self-actualization," "true selves." The power deployed in these films is what Foucault terms "pastoral power," an "individualizing," "salvation oriented" power that "cannot be exercised without knowing the inside of people's minds, without exploring their souls, without making them reveal their innermost secrets" ("Afterword" 214).

We see the exploration of participants' innermost secrets throughout our films as teachers and life coaches incite young people to reveal the traumas of their pasts, making the private public and therefore accessible to remedy and redemption. Within the first minute of *Romeo Is Bleeding*, we see Clark asking the youth in his program, who stand in a line on one side of the room, "Step forward if where you live is not a safe environment for you or your family. Step forward if you have lost someone to gun violence." Nearly all of the students have moved to the other side of the room. In *My Shakespeare*, Patterson Joseph asks his actors, "Anybody who's been stabbed here?" As if to forge a link to the violence of *Romeo and Juliet*, scenes of fight choreography rehearsals are intercut with the narration of Jonathan Taylor, the actor playing Romeo, as he recounts being stabbed twice, once on the lung and once on the spine. Near the end of the film, before the group's performance at RADA, the film's narrator presents us

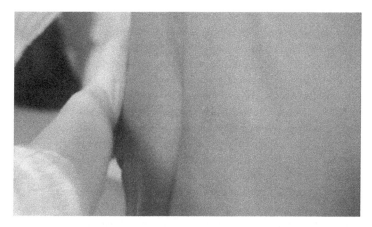

Figure 5 A close-up as Muska discovers Jonathan's scars in *My Shakespeare* (2004)

with an ostensibly private scene, as Muska Khpal, the actor playing Juliet, "emotionally and physically connect[s] with her Romeo ... As she helps Jonathan prepare, she discovers the scars that he received when he was stabbed and almost killed." In an emblematic scene of powerful double-looking, a kind of mise-en-abime holding the dynamics of all our films, we witness her witnessing his wounds. The wounds are shown in close-up (see Figure 5). In *The Hobart Shakespeareans*, after a school lockdown prompted by a nearby shooting, Esquith asks his students: "How many have ever seen violence in your neighborhood? How many of you have problems at home? How many have members of their family who have a drug problem of some kind, alcohol or other kinds of problems? We all have problems. I have them too. Solve them." The shift from second to third person, from "your" to "their," seems significant here, as it indexes the way in which this interrogation and display are not for those in the classroom, all of whom are already familiar with the neighborhood. These appeals are directed at us as viewers, that we might be impressed or moved by the plight of the underdog, that these private facts might become public, and that these problems might be solved or absolved.

Foucault traces how this pastoral power, originating in the church, beginning in the eighteenth century "ceased or at least lost its vitality" as it "spread and multiplied outside of the ecclesiastical institution," suffusing "the family, medicine, psychiatry, education, and employers" ("Afterword" 214, 215). Melinda Cooper, after tracing the resacrilization of social services in the United States, contends that those "versed in the historical taxonomies of Foucault have trouble recognizing that contemporary power might speak the language of moral law, sin, and redemption as much if not more than normativity" (299). The pastoral power operating within the contemporary Shakespeare documentary appears to be bilingual, capable of speaking both languages together in a syncretized dialect. Tanya Erzen, who examines the faith-based prison programs emerging forcefully since Clinton's Charitable Choice legislation, describes what she has termed "testimonial politics": "Testimonial politics rely on redemption narratives in which Evangelical Christians become born-again as new persons ... Testimonial politics emphasize how the experience of becoming a born-again Christian transforms individuals, eliminating the need for social programs focused on structural economic issues" (992). Again, we witness a syncretization of religious and psychoanalytic discourses, a syncretization perhaps best achieved by twentieth- and twenty-first-century self-help culture. And while we might fault the Shakespearean documentary for succumbing to such discourses, alternatives are certainly hard to come by. As Mark Fisher pointedly observes, "A therapeutic narrative of heroic self-transformation is the only story that makes sense in a world in which institutions can no longer be relied upon to support or nurture individuals" ("Anti-therapy" 594). Might there nevertheless be some kind of alternative?

Conclusion

Of all of these contemporary Shakespearean documentaries, one stands out as singular in its approach to teaching and learning. *A Touch of Greatness: A Portrait of a Maverick Teacher* immediately presents itself as unique in four ways. First, the students portrayed are framed as middle class and unexceptional – they're generally not marked as at risk or in need of salvation, and for this reason the film can focus on teaching and learning as ends rather than as means of social uplift. Though the film does explicitly acknowledge racial and religious differences, those differences are not figured as problems to be solved. Second, the film brings together black-and-white 16 mm footage, shot and edited by Robert Downey Sr. in 1964, with footage from a reunion of the students with their teacher Albert Cullum in 1999. This scope shows us what such documentaries looked like before they were shaped by the discourses at work in the films of the late twentieth and early twenty-first centuries, as well as what teaching and learning look like across a lifetime. Third, the pacing of the film – especially the footage from 1964 – has a kind of patience unseen in contemporary documentary counterparts, a patience that more closely mirrors the temporality or duration experienced by those caught up in the day-to-day efforts of teaching and learning. Fourth, whereas most other films seem to frame Shakespearean performance as a means by which students are transformed into responsible adults, this film seems to move in the other direction, bringing out what the film figures as the chaotic immaturity of the plays and their language. At one point in the film Cullum defends himself against accusations that he is "anti-adult" by claiming that he is instead "pro-child." He tells us that the "mystery and magic" of Shakespeare's plays, far from being something one might have to grow to appreciate, are instead what "we adults have lost." While the film does at times slip into confessional modes when students recall being lost and later redeemed by the dramatic performances of the classroom, and while at times some of Cullum's colleagues seem obsessed with "latchkey kids" and "single-parent kids," the film nevertheless eschews narratives of individual transformation and remains primarily focused on curriculum, the power of the arts, and the rewards of child-driven collaborative play.

While the justification for so many of our films, as well as the applied drama they depict, is often rooted in emotional appeals to the transformative potential of empathetic identification, *A Touch of Greatness* seems to hold audiences at a slight remove. The students do not weep, and we do not weep for them. They are not underdogs, and Mr. Cullum does not save them. Empathy and identification – and their discontents – organize a long history of debate on the effects of drama, from Aristotle's *Poetics* to Brecht, from Boal to Jessica Bauman's recent citation of Lin-Manuel Miranda's description of theater as an "empathy machine." In many ways, empathy is the ground upon which therapeutic discourses flourish, from Freud to today's evangelists of self-help culture, from the moralizing pedagogues of the nineteenth century to those designing today's character education curricula. We find an ostensibly politicized empathy in conservative calls to "rally the armies of compassion" – Bush's rallying cry on the occasion of his creation of the Office of Faith-Based and Community Initiatives – wherein empathy substitutes for and displaces more comprehensive forms of systemic support and care (*Rallying* 4). Illouz has traced the rise of empathy as a desired occupational capacity, from Mayo's workplace interventions to the current vogue of emotional intelligence (*Saving* 80).

But empathy has its critics. Susan Sontag's *Regarding the Pain of Others* insightfully sketches out the limits of empathy as it relates to photography, and many of her insights are useful when thinking about the contemporary underdog documentary. Sontag writes, "Compassion is an unstable emotion. It needs to be translated into action, or it withers" (101). In the field of psychology, Paul Bloom has received much attention for his provocative study *Against Empathy: A Case for Rational Compassion*, wherein he argues, "Your empathy doesn't drive your moral evaluation of [others]. Rather, it's your moral evaluation of the person that determines whether or not you feel empathy" (70). Echoing Sontag, Bloom contends that empathy can be very unstable, narrow, and easily manipulated (9). Bloom claims that because empathy "focuses on specific individuals," it tends to obscure larger political contexts (31). He points to the case of school shootings, which, although "statistically insignificant" in relation to other forms of gun violence, stoke empathy and emotion. Bloom describes the Newtown massacre, in particular, as a case in which "people from far poorer communities [were] sending their money to much richer people, guided by the persistent itch of empathetic concern" (32). Megan Boler, in her critique of Aristotle, argues that empathy more often than not results in a "projection of myself more than an understanding of you." She asks a crucial question: "What is gained and/or lost by advocating as a cure for social injustice an empathetic identification that is more about me than you?" (159). She cites an unnamed colleague, who points out what should perhaps be obvious, that "these 'others' whose lives we imagine don't want empathy, they want justice" (157). Even as the popular press attempts to resuscitate a beleaguered humanities by focusing on literature's ability to foster empathetic relations, critics within literary studies have also begun sketching out the limits of empathy. Rachel Greenwald Smith's *Affect and American Literature in the Age of Neoliberalism* acknowledges that literature "interacts with us, it changes us, and sometimes might even do so for the better." However, she claims that it will do so "not by the cultivation of empathy or any other recognizable sentiment, but by alerting us to the possibility that there are forms of knowledge that we do not yet know and forms of feeling that we cannot yet feel" (126).

The idea that empathetic identifications are less about justice and more about ego is perhaps nowhere better illustrated than within the *Henriad* itself. The role-playing that Falstaff and Hal do, a kind of applied drama if you will, with each taking on the role of Hal's father in order to serve their own purposes, might offer one example one example of the uses and abuses of empathy. Another telling moment comes when the Chief Justice, anticipating Hal's revenge now that he has literally taken his father's place on the throne, proposes a kind of empathy game, one that again asks Hal to place himself, emotionally, into his father's place:

> Be now the father, and propose a son,
> Hear your own dignity so much profan'd,
> See your most dreadful laws so loosely slighted,
> Behold yourself so by a son distain'd:
> And then imagine me taking your part,
> And in your power soft silencing your son. (*2H4* 5.2.92–5.2.97)

Hal does, in this empathetic game, move outside of himself and take on the Chief Justice's and his father's perspectives, prompting him to identify with the law and decide against his own interests. But as he advises Falstaff, we should "Presume not that [he] is the thing [he] was" (5.5.56). His interests have shifted. As Falstaff learns too late, empathy, a fickle thing in and of itself, can easily shift and in no way necessarily gravitates toward justice.

While Albert Cullum, like so many others, stresses the need to build student self-esteem or the need for students to be "emotionally honest" when performing, his students do seem to use performance as a means of moving beyond themselves. Many former students recall making connections between the plays they performed – by Shakespeare, Shaw, Sophocles, and others – and larger social issues. Unlike most of these films, which seem intent on teaching youth to respect authority and be compliant when commanded, *A Touch of Greatness* depicts an environment in which both teacher and students collectively deploy emotion against the status quo, engaging in behaviors that index a link between performance and protest not yet recuperated by the discourses over-determining the rest of our films. Anne Stillman remembers that the most important role she played was that of Antigone. Her recollections are intercut with striking 16 mm footage of her classmates performing *Antigone* on the beach (see Figure 6):

> She was such a strong figure, who was willing to stand up to
> the authorities even when it was punishable by death . . . At
> the time I played that role, you know, we were children in

Figure 6 *Antigone* on the beach in *A Touch of Greatness* (2004)

the 60s, and there were very real parallels with the civil rights movement. I knew that there were people who were being beaten and in some cases killed for what they believed and for trying to right a wrong. And I've never forgotten that sort of very young experience of playing this person who was willing to defy every authority in order to do what she felt was right.

We also meet David Pugh, who was a "troublemaker" before entering Cullum's class in 1959. The film follows Pugh in 1999, now a teacher working in an alternative school in NYC, as he teaches classes populated by "wonderful kids," all of whom are students of color, who "deserve much better than they're getting." Pugh cites Cullum as an inspiration, but acknowledges that the latter's techniques, however, need to be "converted to a new reality." He discusses systemic problems in schools: the emphasis on testing, tracking, and segregating schools by race and class, all of which prepare different students for varied and unequal futures.

Near the end of *A Touch of Greatness*, Cullum explains, "I think teaching is pushing them away from you, through doors, different doors, not embracing them. When you embrace someone, you're holding them back." He then provides an emblem for his teaching philosophy by describing Picasso's *Mother & Child* (1921) (see Figure 7). In the painting, he tells us, the mother is "balancing the baby perfectly. She doesn't hold him. He's balanced. He can go any time he's capable of going. But he's perfectly balanced until he takes a step. Classroom teaching should be that. Find a security spot for them, and then they're ready to go."

Cullum's reading of Picasso's painting brings to mind D. W. Winnicott's formulation of the "good-enough mother," a parent who supports, yet slowly withdraws the environmental conditions fostering a child's primary narcissism. As these supports are slowly withdrawn and replaced by new, transitional, and external supports (Winnicott importantly names the arts as one such replacement), the individuated child develops a limited and contingent autonomy (18).

Figure 7 Picasso's *Mother & Child* (1921)

Surprisingly, David Whitman also turns to Winnicott's good-enough mother in *Sweating the Small Stuff*. But his reading is colored by his anxiety about absent fathers, which he reads into Winnicott when he decries what he calls a "yawning gap in the key child development theory of the 'good-enough' mother." The new paternalists are fond of saying that "developmental" models tailor schools to fit students, whereas students should be shaped to fit schools. Against the developmental model, with its good-enough mothering, Whitman suggests the model of the "good-enough father": "Like today's paternalistic schools, the good-enough father might be described as the guardian of adolescents who brings structure and discipline to their lives but ultimately encourages the development of a sense of mastery and self-sufficiency ... The good-enough father thus aims to preempt misbehavior and inculcate middle-class mores by teaching children to 'act right,' much as paternalistic schools do" (*Sweating* 43).

But Whitman's engagement with Winnicott – his intervention – is disingenuous. Winnicott's good-enough mother isn't necessarily even gendered in the way Whitman imagines. Martha Nussbaum tells us that Winnicott "did increasingly stress that 'mother' was a role rather than a biological category, that real mothers had aspects of both genders, and that analysts, biologically male and female, typically play a quasi-maternal role" (384). Though he does equivocate at times, Winnicott pretty straight-forwardly states of the good-enough mother that "[t]his includes fathers" (*Sweating* 191). Beyond issues of gender, though these are certainly important for him, Whitman's engagement with Winnicott is also disingenuous because he disregards the latter's emphasis on what he called "the facilitating environment," a crucial infrastructure of support upon which children may flourish. The neoliberal aspirations of the new paternalists, shifting as they do the provisions of care from public to private hands, making no excuses for individual failure in the face of systemic deprivations, might instead be imagined as those fostering a "debilitating environment." Winnicott calls the facilitating environment a "continuity of care," arguing that such continued support and care is the antithesis of "a pattern of reacting to the unpredictable and for ever [*sic*] starting again," exactly the kind of neoliberal precarity to which new paternalism seeks to inure our children (191).

Social services – from welfare to social security to health care to the arts – make up such a facilitating environment, but such an environment need not, according to the logic of empathy (and some logics of "community"), erase distinctions or differences between members. Nussbaum writes of Winnicott that he "attached particular importance to the arts, which help people under social pressure (as all people ultimately are) to keep on enriching their sense of the 'potential space' between individuals" (185). Cullum likewise argues for space where so many of our films aim to reduce it. The double-looking structure adopted by our documentaries tends to operate according to a logic of empathetic nearness: through abstract analogies, students will erase the distance between themselves and Shakespeare's historical characters; teachers, like Rancière's stultifying pedagogue, will strive to erase the gap between what they know and what their students know; and we, as viewers, will empathetically identify with both the films' underdogs and those who redeem them. Against this logic of empathic identification, philosopher Katja Haustein advocates for what she calls "tact": "Although the ability to empathize may provide a route to tactful behavior, tact, unlike empathy, does not aim at nearness. On the contrary, its goal is . . . to generate distance and to acknowledge difference . . . tact, unlike empathy, is often associated with discretion and respect for the space of the other" (2–3).

In Cullum's classroom, tact involves entering into imaginative worlds with students rather than disciplining and training them in the ways of adulthood. Roland Barthes writes of children's toys that they "*literally* prefigure the world" of adults, as if "in the eyes of the public the child was, all told, nothing but a smaller man" (53). Barthes bemoans the rarity of "invented forms" not designed to turn children into adult property owners (53). In Cullum's class, the plays of Shakespeare and others – anything, really – take on the shape and function of such plastic or poetic forms. Within the first minute of the film, we see Cullum and his students stacking a precarious pile of six chairs atop a table. These chairs, we learn, represent Pike's Peak. The students watch in anticipation as the structure topples. Then, we see Cullum unfurl a massive ream of butcher paper, hundreds of feet long, across a playground. The paper, in this game, represents the Mississippi River. The students, in their bathing suits, proceed to swim across the paper river. Then, the students are seen pushing the river through the classroom window into the room (see Figure 8). A young boy explains in voiceover: "We were pulling the Mississippi River in the classroom. It almost went all the way around the room." Cullum replies, "I think it's the first time a river has entered a classroom." Laurie Heineman recalls an engagement with ballet that couldn't be more different than those depicted in *Ballet Changed My Life*: "I used to be in ballet club. [Cullum] ran ballet club. He wasn't ever trying to be a ballet teacher. He didn't teach us how to do it properly, how to, you know, 'first position, second position.' He put on music and came up with stories, and we danced the stories, and we danced with such freedom and joy. I think it was the best dancing I ever did." In another scene, kindergarten students perform the roles of the fairies in

Figure 8 The Mississippi River enters the classroom

Midsummer Night's Dream. Mr. Cullum feeds the students marshmallows (see Figure 9). A student in voiceover tells us, "They're eating marshmallows so they will be light as fairies, so that they can hop and jump around in the snow, and they won't have any trouble acting out their parts … And each time they do it, it's different, and you never know what's going to happen because they just dance as they feel like it." Another student chimes in, "It always comes out very well."

The students in *Touch of Greatness* go to school in suburban Rye, New York, and they, unlike the students in the other films, rest assured in their community's facilitating environment. Because of this, their engagement with the arts and humanities performs differently. Because the arts and humanities, like other forms of social welfare, are under siege, one might therefore argue that now is not the time to critique their power to transform lives. However, I would argue that now more than ever we should resist

Figure 9 Mr. Cullum feeds kindergarteners marshmallows

representations in which the arts and humanities are wielded as cudgels to better shape future workers or as a spiritual force sent to redeem a pathologized and sinful underclass. We might instead try to imagine the arts and humanities' power to invent new ways of being and performing together, ways in which difference or particularity need not be erased in the name of some homogenous culture of excellence. I hope we see future films in which the full potential of the humanities is engaged. These films do not yet exist, but *A Touch of Greatness* does signal a way forward.

References

Adorno, Theodor. *Minima Moralia: Reflections from Damaged Life*. Translated by E. F. N. Jephcott. Verso, 2005.

Ahmed, Sara. *The Cultural Politics of Emotion*. Second ed. Edinburg University Press, 2014.

Althusser, Louis. *Lenin and Philosophy and Other Essays*. Translated by Ben Brewster. Monthly Review Press, 2001.

Aronsky, Rory L. "The Hobart Shakespeareans." Film Threat, Mar. 30, 2006. http://filmthreat.com/uncategorized/the-hobart-shakespeareans-dvd/

Arthur, James, Kristján Kristjánsson, David Walker, Wouter Sanderse, Chantel Jones, with Stephen Thoma, Randal Curren, and Michael Roberts. "Character Education in UK Schools: Research Report." Jubilee Centre for Character and Virtues, University of Birmingham, Feb. 2015. www.jubileecentre.ac.uk

Arts Midwest. "Shakespeare in American Communities." www.artsmidwest .org/programs/shakespeare

Autism Self Advocacy Network. "Disability Community Condemns Autism Speaks." Autistic Advocacy.org, Oct. 7, 2009. https://autisticadvocacy .org/2009/10/disability-community-condemns-autism-speaks/

Baker, Bruce and Gary Miron. *The Business of Charter Schooling: Understanding the Policies That Charter Operators Use for Financial Benefit*. National Education Policy Center, 2015.

Ballet Saved My Life: Ballet-Hoo! Directed by Claire Lasko and Michael Waldman. Diverse Bristol TV, 2006.

Barthes, Roland. *Mythologies*. Translated by Annette Lavers. Hill and Wang, 1972.

Bauman, Jessica. "What Refugees Taught Me about Shakespeare." (TEDxCU NY), Jun. 14, 2018. www.youtube.com/watch?v=mj5nDKXyxL0

Ben-Ishai, Elizabeth. "The New Paternalism: An Analysis of Power, State Intervention, and Autonomy." *Policy Research Quarterly*, vol. 65, no. 1, pp. 151–165.

Berlant, Lauren. *Cruel Optimism*. Duke University Press, 2011.

"The Subject of True Feeling: Pain, Privacy, and Politics." *Cultural Pluralism, Identity Politics, and the Law*. Edited by Austin Sarat and Thomas R. Kearns. University of Michigan Press, 1999, pp. 49–84.

Bishop, Claire. *Artificial Hells: Participatory Arts and the Politics of Spectatorship*. Verso, 2012.

Bloom, Paul. *Against Empathy: A Case for Rational Compassion*. Ecco, 2018.

Blume, Howard. "L.A. Unified Settles Lawsuits with Teacher Rafe Esquith." *Los Angeles Times*, Sept. 13, 2017. www.latimes.com/local/lanow/la-me-edu-rafe-esquith-settlement-20170912-story.html

Boal, Augusto. *Theatre of the Oppressed*, 1979. Translated by Charles A. and Maria-Odilia Leal McBride. Theatre Communications Group, 1985.

Boler, Megan. *Feeling Power: Emotions and Education*. Routledge, 1999.

Bowles, Samuel and Herbert Gintis. "*Schooling in Capitalist America* Revisited." *Sociology of Education*, vol. 75, no. 2, 2002, pp. 1–18.

Bristol, Michael D. *Shakespeare's America, America's Shakespeare*. Routledge, 1990.

Brown, Wendy. *Undoing the Demos: Neoliberalism's Stealth Revolution*. Zone, 2015.

Burke, Kenneth. "Why *A Midsummer Night's Dream*?" 1972. *Kenneth Burke on Shakespeare*. Edited by Scott L. Newstok. Parlor Press, 2007, pp. 172–186.

Bush, George W. *Rallying the Armies of Compassion: Message from the President of the United States, Transmitting a Report to Support the Heroic Works of Faith-Based and Community Groups across America*. House Document 107–36. US Government Printing Office, Jan. 31, 2001.

"Remarks at the White House Conference on Character and Community, June 19, 2002." *Public Papers of the Presidents of the*

United States: George W. Bush. US Government Printing Office, 2004, pp. 1020–1022.

Butts, R. Freeman. "The Politics of Civic and Moral Education." *Civic and Moral Learning in America.* Edited by Donald Warren and John J. Patrick. Palgrave, 2006, pp. 7–19.

Caesar Must Die (Cesare deve morire). Directed by Paolo and Vittorio Taviani. Kaos Cinematografica, 2012.

Chaudhuri, Sukanta, editor. "Introduction." *William Shakespeare's* A Midsummer Night's Dream. Bloomsbury Arden, 2017, pp. 1–117.

Cole, Teju. "The White-Savior Industrial Complex." *The Atlantic,* Mar. 21, 2012. theatlantic.com/international/archive/2012/03/the-white-savior-industrial-complex/254843/

Cooper, Melinda. *Family Values: Between Neoliberalism and the New Social Conservatism.* Zone Books, 2017.

Craik, T. W., editor. "Introduction." *William Shakespeare's* Henry V. 1995. Arden Shakespeare, 2000, pp. 1–111.

Credé, Marcus, Michael C. Tynan, and Peter D. Harms. "Much Ado about Grit: A Meta-Analytic Synthesis of the Grit Literature." *Journal of Personality and Social Psychology,* vol. 113, no. 3, 2017, pp. 492–551.

Daniel-Braham, Will. "Will Daniel-Braham." Life Coach Directory. life coach-directory.org.uk/lifecoaches/will-daniel-braham

Dornfield, Ann. "Students Pay 'Rent' or Lose Their Desks at This Elementary School." KUOW.org, Mar. 15, 2019. kuow.org/stories/students-pay-rent-or-lose-their-desks-at-this-covington-elementary-school

Duckworth, Angela. *Grit: The Power of Passion and Perseverance.* Scribner, 2016.

Empson, William. *Some Versions of the Pastoral.* New Directions, 1974.

Erickson, Megan. *Class War: The Privatization of Childhood.* Verso, 2015.

Erzen, Tanya. "Testimonial Politics: The Christian Right's Faith-Based Approach to Marriage and Imprisonment." *American Quarterly*, vol. 59, no. 3, Sept. 2007, pp. 991–1015.

Esquith, Rafe. "There Are No Shortcuts." Lavin Agency, Nov. 2004. web .archive.org/web/ 20040301202849/ http:www.thelavinagency.com /usa/rafeesquith.html.

Fisher, Mark. "Anti-therapy." *K-Punk: The Collected and Unpublished Writings of Mark Fisher (2004–2016)*. Edited by Darren Ambrose. Repeater Books, 2018, pp. 589–598.

    Capitalist Realism: Is There No Alternative? Zero Books, 2009.

    K-Punk: The Collected and Unpublished Writings of Mark Fisher (2004–2016). Edited by Darren Ambrose. Repeater Books, 2018.

    "Suffering with a Smile." *K-Punk: The Collected and Unpublished Writings of Mark Fisher (2004–2016)*. Edited by Darren Ambrose. Repeater Books, 2018, pp. 535–537.

"Focus on Character." Knowledge Is Power Program. www.kipp.org /approach/character/

Foucault, Michel. "The Subject and Power." Afterword. *Michel Foucault: Beyond Structuralism and Hermeneutics*, 1982. Edited by Hubert L. Dreyfus and Paul Rabinow. Second ed. University of Chicago Press, 1983.

    Discipline and Punish: The Birth of the Prison, 1977. Translated by Alan Sheridan. Second ed. Vintage Books, 1995.

    History of Sexuality: Volume I: An Introduction, 1978. Translated by Robert Hurley. Vintage Books, 1990.

Freire, Paulo. *Pedagogy of the Oppressed*, 1970. New revised twentieth-anniversary ed. Translated by Myra Bergman Ramos. Continuum, 1998.

Frey, Charles. "Teaching Shakespeare in America." *Shakespeare Quarterly*, vol. 35, no. 5. Special Issue: Teaching Shakespeare, 1984, pp. 541–559.

Gioia, Dana. "Chairman's Message." *Shakespeare in American Communities*. National Endowment for the Arts Publication, 2005, p. 1.

"Introduction for Teachers." *Shakespeare in American Communities: A Special Audio Program for Teachers*. Narrated by Dana Gioia. National Endowment for the Arts / Arts Midwest, 2011. CD.

Giroux, Henry A. *The Abandoned Generation: Democracy beyond the Culture of Fear*. Palgrave, 2003.

Glanzer, Perry L. and Andrew J. Milson. "Legislating the Good: A Survey and Evaluation of Character Education Laws in the United States." *Education Policy*, vol. 20, no. 3, Jul. 2006, pp. 525–550.

Godmilow, Jill. "What's Wrong with the Liberal Documentary." *Peace Review*, vol. 11, no. 1, 1999, pp. 91–98.

Goffman, Erving. *The Presentation of Self in Everyday Life*. Anchor Books, 1959.

Graff, Gerald. *Professing Literature: An Institutional History*. Chicago University Press, 1987.

Greene, Peter. "How to Profit from Your Nonprofit Charter School." *Forbes*, Aug. 13, 2018. www.forbes.com/sites/petergreene/2018/08/13/how-to-profit-from-your-non-profit-charter-school/

"Report: The Department of Education Has Spent \$1 Billion on Charter Waste and Fraud." *Forbes*, May 29, 2019. www.forbes.com/sites/peter greene/2019/03/29/report-the-department-of-education-has-spent-1-bil lion-on-charter-school-waste-and-fraud/

Greenhalgh, Susanne and Robert Shaughnessy. "Our Shakespeare: British Television and the Strains of Multiculturalism." *Screening Shakespeare in the Twenty-First Century*. Edited by Mark Thornton Burnett and Ramona Wray. Edinburgh University Press, 2006, pp. 90–112.

Greenwald Smith, Rachel. *Affect and American Literature in the Age of Neoliberalism*. Cambridge University Press, 2015.

Han, Byung-Chul. *Psychopolitics: Neoliberalism and New Technologies of Power*. Verso, 2017.

Hartocollis, Anemona. "Michael Feinberg, a Founder of KIPP Schools, Is Fired after Misconduct Claims." *New York Times*, Feb. 22, 2018. www.nytimes .com/2018/02/22/us/kipp-sexual-misconduct-michael-feinberg.html

Haustein, Katja. "How to Be Alone with Others: Plessner, Adorno, and Barthes on Tact." *Modern Language Review*, vol. 114, no. 1, January 2019, pp. 1–21.

Hindmarsh, D. Bruce. *The Evangelical Conversion Narrative: Spiritual Autobiography in Early Modern England*. Oxford University Press, 2005.

The Hobart Shakespeareans. Directed by Mel Stuart, 2005; POV/PBS, 2006.

Hochschild, Arlie Russell. *The Managed Heart: Commercialization of Human Feeling*, 1983. University of California Press, 2012.

Howard, Robert W. Marvin W. Berkowitz, and Esther F. Schaeffer, "Politics of Character Education." *Educational Policy*, vol. 18, no. 1, 2004, pp. 188–215.

Hughes, Jenny and Helen Nicholson. "Applied Theatre: Ecology of Practices." *Critical Perspectives on Applied Theatre*. Edited by Jenny Hughes and Helen Nicholson. Cambridge University Press, 2016, pp. 1–12.

Illouz, Eva. *Cold Intimacies: The Making of Emotional Capitalism*. Polity Press, 2007.

Oprah Winfrey and the Clamour of Misery: An Essay on Popular Culture. Columbia University Press, 2003.

Saving the Modern Soul: Therapy, Emotions, and the Culture of Self-Help. University of California Press, 2008.

Jail Caesar. Directed by Paul Schoolman. Caesar Productions, 2012.

Kahana, Jonathan. *Intelligence Work: The Politics of American Documentary*. Columbia University Press, 2008.

"Introduction to Section VI." *The Documentary Film Reader: History, Theory, Criticism*. Edited by Jonathan Kahana. Oxford University Press, 2016, pp. 723–725.

Kahana, Jonathan, editor. *The Documentary Film Reader: History, Theory, Criticism*. Oxford University Press, 2016.

Kestenbaum, Sam. "The Curious Mystical Text behind Marianne Williamson's Presidential Bid." *New York Times*, Jul. 5, 2019. www .nytimes.com/2019/07/05/nyregion/marianne-williamson.html

Kings of Baxter: Can Twelve Teenage Offenders Conquer Macbeth? Directed by Jack Yabsley. Grumpy Sailor, 2017.

Kumashiro, Kevin K. "Wrong Choice for Secretary of Education: A Dissenting Voice from Chicago." *Education Week*, Jan. 12, 2009. www .edweek.org/ew/articles/2009/01/12/ 18kumashiro-com.h28.html

La Berge, Leigh Claire and Quinn Slobodian. "Reading for Neoliberalism, Reading Like Neoliberals." *American Literary History*, vol. 29, no. 3, 2017, pp. 602–614.

Lanier, Douglas M. "Shakescorp Noir." *Shakespeare Quarterly*, vol. 53, no. 2, 2002, pp. 157–180.

Laporte, Charles. "The Bard, the Bible, and the Victorian Shakespeare Question." *ELH*, vol. 74, no. 3, Fall 2007, pp. 609–628.

Lickona, Thomas. "Religion and Character Education." *Phi Delta Kappan*, vol. 81, no. 1, Sept. 1999, pp. 21+.

Looking for Richard. Directed by Al Pacino. Twentieth Century Fox, 1996.

McGee, Micki. *Self-Help, Inc.: Makeover Culture in American Life*. Oxford University Press, 2005.

Mead, Lawrence, editor. *The New Paternalism: Supervisory Approaches to Poverty*. Brookings Institution Press, 1997.

Mickey B. Directed by Tom Magill. Educational Shakespeare Company, 2007.

Midsummer in Newtown. Directed by Lloyd Kramer. Vulcan Productions, 2016.

Mintz, Steven. "Michael More and the Re-birth of the Documentary." *Film & History*, vol. 35, no. 2, 2005, pp. 10–11.

Miron, Gary and Charisse Gulosino. *Profiles of For-Profit and Nonprofit Education Management Organizations: Fourteenth Annual Report 2011–2012*. National Education Policy Center, 2013.

Montrose, Louis Adrian. "Of Gentlemen and Shepherds: The Politics of Elizabethan Pastoral Form." *ELH*, vol. 50, no. 3, Autumn 1983, pp. 415–459.

Morse, Ruth. "*The Hollow Crown*: Shakespeare, the BBC, and the 2012 London Olympics." *Linguaculture*, vol. 1, 2014, pp. 7–20.

Murray, Susan. "'I Think We Need a New Name for It': The Meeting of Documentary and Reality TV." *Reality TV: Remaking Television Culture*. 2004. Edited by Susan Murray and Laurie Ouellette. New York University Press, 2009, pp. 65–81.

Murray, Susan and Laurie Ouellette. "Introduction." *Reality TV: Remaking Television Culture*. 2004. Edited by Susan Murray and Laurie Ouellette. New York University Press, 2009, pp. 1–20.

Murray, Susan and Laurie Ouellette, editors. *Reality TV: Remaking Television Culture*. 2004. New York University Press, 2009.

My Classroom Economy. "Overview." The Vanguard Group. myclassroomeconomy.org/overview.html

My Shakespeare: Romeo and Juliet for a New Generation with Baz Luhrmann. Directed by Michael Waldman. Penguin Television, 2004.

National Endowment for the Arts. "2008 Guide." Jan. 2008.

    "About Shakespeare in American Communities." www.arts.gov/national/shakespeare/about

    "National Endowment for the Arts Announces Star-Studded 'Player's Guild' for *Shakespeare in American Communities*." https://web.archive.org/web/20120514134300/http://nea.gov/national/shakespeare/Guild.html

"National Endowment for the Arts Appropriations History." www.arts
.gov/open-government/national-endowment-arts-appropriations-
history

Nelson, Maggie. *The Art of Cruelty: A Reckoning*. Norton, 2011.

Newstok (Newstrom), Scott. "Right Pitches Dubya As Henry V."
Alternet, May 29, 2003. www.alternet.org/2003/05/right_pitches_
dubya_as_henry_v/

Nichols, Bill. *Representing Reality: Issues and Concepts in Documentary*.
Indiana University Press, 1991.

Nicholson, Helen. *Applied Drama: The Gift of Theatre*. 2005. Second ed.
Palgrave, 2014.

Nietzsche, Friedrich. "The Problem of Socrates." *Twilight of the Idols/The
Anti-Christ*. Translated by R. J. Hollingdale. Penguin, 1990, pp. 39–44.

Notes from the Field. Directed by Kristi Zea. HBO Films, 2018.

Nussbaum, Martha. "Winnicott on the Surprises of the Self." *Massachusetts
Review*, vol. 47, no. 2, The Messy Self, Summer 2006, pp. 375–393.

O'Dair, Sharon. *Class, Critics, and Shakespeare: Bottom Lines on the Culture
Wars*, 2000. University of Michigan Press, 2003.

Office of the Press Secretary. "President Holds Press Conference." News
release, Oct. 28, 2003. whitehouse.gov/news/releases/2003/
10/20031028–2.html

Olive, Sarah. "'In Shape and Mind Transformed'? Televised Teaching and
Learning Shakespeare." *Palgrave Communications*, vol. 2, no. 16608,
April 5, 2016.

Ouellette, Laurie and James Hay. *Better Living through Reality TV:
Television and Post-Welfare Citizenship*. Blackwell, 2008.

"Piss in One's Pocket." Urban Dictionary. www.urbandictionary.com

Pozner, Jennifer L. *Reality Bites Back: The Troubling Truth about Guilty
Pleasure TV*. Seal Press, 2010.

Purcell, Stephen. "Shakespeare on Television." *Edinburgh Companion to Shakespeare and the Arts*. Edited by Mark Thornton Burnett, Adrian Streete, and Ramona Wray. Edinburgh University Press, pp. 522–540.

Rancière, Jacques. *The Emancipated Spectator*. Translated by Gregory Elliott. Verso, 2009.

Rangan, Pooja. *Immediations: The Humanitarian Impulse in Documentary*. Duke University Press, 2017.

Raphael, Chad. "The Political Economic Origins of Reali-TV." *Reality TV: Remaking Television Culture*. 2004. Edited by Susan Murray and Laurie Ouellette.New York University Press, 2009, pp. 123–140.

Ravitch, Diane. *The Death and Life of the Great American School System: How Testing and Choice Are Undermining Education*. Revised and expanded ed. Basic Books, 2011.

Readings, Bill. *The University in Ruins*. Harvard University Press, 1996.

Renaissance Man. Directed by Penny Marshall. Touchstone Pictures, 1994.

Romeo Is Bleeding. Directed by Jason Zeldes. Leo Persham Pictures, 2015.

Sanchez, Melissa E. "'Use Me But as Your Spaniel': Feminism, Queer Theory, and Early Modern Sexualities," *PMLA*, vol. 127, no. 3, May 2012, pp. 493–451.

"Self-Control." Character Lab. https://characterlab.org/playbooks/self-control/

Sennett, Richard. *The Culture of the New Capitalism*. Yale University Press, 2006.

Serpe, Nick. "Reality Pawns: The New Money TV." *Dissent*, vol. 60, no. 3, Summer 2013, pp. 13–18.

Shakespeare Behind Bars. Directed by Hank Rogerson. Philomath Films, 2005.

Shakespeare High. Directed by Alex Rotaru. Trigger Street Productions, 2011.

Shakespeare, William. *The First Part of King Henry IV*. Edited by A. R. Humphreys. Thomson Learning / Arden Shakespeare, 2000.

  King Henry V. 1995. Edited by T. W. Craik. Thomson Learning / Arden Shakespeare, 2000.

  Midsummer Night's Dream. Edited by Sukanta Chaudhuri. Bloomsbury / Arden Shakespeare, 2017.

  Othello. Revised ed. Edited by E. A. J. Honigmann. Bloomsbury / Arden Shakespeare, 2016.

  The Second Part of King Henry IV. Edited by A. R. Humphreys. Meuthen / Arden Shakespeare, 1966.

Shirley, Don. "County Wants Shakespeare Fest Out, Out of July Spot." *Los Angeles Times*, Oct. 31, 1993, p. 46.

Smagorinsky, Peter and Joel Taxel. *The Discourse of Character Education: Culture Wars in the Classroom*. Lawrence Erlbaum Associates, 2005.

Sontag, Susan. *Regarding the Pain of Others*. Picador, 2003.

Soss, Joe, Richard C. Fording, and Sanford F. Schram. *Disciplining the Poor: Neoliberal Paternalism and the Persistent Power of Race*. University of Chicago Press, 2011.

Spillers, Hortense J. "Mama's Baby, Papa's Maybe: An American Grammar Book." *Diacritics*, vol. 17, no. 2, Summer 1987, pp. 64–81.

Starobin, Paul. "The Daddy State." *National Journal*, vol. 30, no. 13, Mar. 28, 1998, pp. 678–683.

Strauss, Valerie. "The World's Most Famous Teacher Blasts School Reform." *Washington Post*, Jul. 16, 2013.

Thompson, Ayanna. *Passing Strange: Shakespeare, Race, and Contemporary America*. Oxford University Press, 2011.

Thompson, Ayanna and Laura Turchi. *Teaching Shakespeare with Purpose: A Student-Centered Approach*. 2016. Bloomsbury / Arden Shakespeare, 2018.

Torres, Zahira and Howard Blume. "Rafe Esquith Fired: Former Teacher of the Year Accused of Inappropriately Touching Minors." *Los Angeles Times*, Oct. 14, 2015. www.latimes.com/local/education/la-me-esquith-20151015-story.html

A Touch of Greatness: A Portrait of a Maverick Teacher. Directed by Leslie Sullivan. Aubin Pictures, 2004.

US Department of Labor. *The Negro Family: A Case for National Action*. US Government Printing Office, 1965.

Verhoeven, Beatrice. "Writers Guild East Slams Reality TV Shows As 'High-Status Sweatshops.'" The Wrap, Apr. 26, 2017. www.thewrap.com/wga-east-slams-reality-tv-shows-as-high-status-sweatshops-more-rights-for-writers/

Wacquant, Loïc. *Punishing the Poor: The Neoliberal Government of Social Insecurity*. Duke University Press, 2009.

Wade, Laura. *Posh*. Oberon, 2010.

Watts, Amber. "Melancholy, Merit, and Merchandise: The Postwar Audience Participation Show." *Reality TV: Remaking Television Culture*. 2004. Edited by Susan Murray and Laurie Ouellette. New York University Press, 2009, pp. 301–320.

Watz, Michael. "An Historical Analysis of Character Education." *Journal of Inquiry & Action in Education*, vol. 4, no. 2, 2011, pp. 34–53.

Whitman, David. "David Whitman: Sweating the Small Stuff." Fora.tv, episode 1114, part of the Koret Foundation's Principles of a Free Society series, The Commonwealth Club of California, 2008.

Sweating the Small Stuff: Inner-City Schools and the New Paternalism. Thomas B. Fordham Institute, 2008.

Wilhelm, Ian. "The Rise of Charity TV." *Chronicle of Philanthropy*, vol. 19, no. 8, Feb. 8, 2007, p. 24.

Williams, Linda. "Mirrors without Memories: Truth, History, and the New Documentary," 1993. *The Documentary Film Reader: History, Theory,*

Criticism. Edited by Jonathan Kahana.Oxford University Press, 2016, pp. 794–806.

Willis, Sharon. *The Poitier Effect: Racial Melodrama and Fantasies of Reconciliation*. University of Minnesota Press, 2015.

Winnicott, D. W. *Playing and Reality*, 1971. Routledge Classics, 2005.

Winston, Brian. "The Tradition of the Victim in Griersonian Documentary," 1988. *The Documentary Film Reader: History, Theory, Criticism*. Edited by Jonathan Kahana. Oxford University Press, 2016, pp. 762–775.

Why Shakespeare? Directed by Lawrence Bridges. Red Car, 2005.

Cambridge Elements ☰

Shakespeare Performance

W. B. Worthen
Barnard College

W. B. Worthen is Alice Brady Pels Professor in the Arts, and
Chair of the Theatre Department at Barnard College. He is also
co-chair of the Ph.D. Program in Theatre at Columbia
University, where he is Professor of English and Comparative
Literature.

Cambridge Elements ≡

Shakespeare Performance

CPSIA information can be obtained
at www.ICGtesting.com
Printed in the USA
LVHW031931020420
652037LV00009B/208

9 781108 743167